Bikepacking King Alfred's Way

353km gravel loop from Winchester

by Ed Hunton

JUNIPER HOUSE, MURLEY MOSS,
OXENHOLME ROAD, KENDAL, CUMBRIA LA9 7RL
www.cicerone.co.uk

© Ed Hunton 2026
First edition 2026
ISBN: 978 1 78631 238 9
eISBN: 978 1 78765 228 6

Printed in Singapore by KHL Printing using responsibly sourced paper.
A catalogue record for this book is available from the British Library.
All photographs are by the author unless otherwise stated.

 Route mapping by Lovell Johns lovelljohns.com

NASA relief data courtesy of ESRI
King Alfred's Way © 2026 Cyclists Touring Club trading as Cycling UK™. All rights reserved
Cicerone's EU representative for GPSR compliance is Easy Access System Europe, Mustamäe tee 50, 10621 Tallinn, Estonia. Email gpsr.requests@easproject.com.

For Nicky Stoupe

Updates to this guide

While every effort is made by our authors to ensure the accuracy of guidebooks as they go to print, changes can occur during the lifetime of an edition. Any updates that we know of for this guide will be on the Cicerone website (cicerone.co.uk/1238/updates), so please check before planning your trip. We also advise that you check information about such things as transport, accommodation and shops locally. Even rights of way can be altered over time. We are always grateful for information about any discrepancies between a guidebook and the facts on the ground, sent by email to updates@cicerone.co.uk.

Register your book: To sign up to receive free updates, special offers and GPX files where available, create a Cicerone account and register your purchase via the 'My Account' tab at cicerone.co.uk.

Front cover: Descending White Horse Hill (Stage 4)

Contents

Map key 4
Route summary table 6
Alternative schedules: wild camping 8
Alternative schedules: campsites 10
Alternative schedules: hostels and B&Bs 12

Introduction 15

What is bikepacking?. 16
Planning your ride 17
What to take 19
Rights of way 20
Navigation 21
Accommodation 21
Fuel strategies 22
About the route 23
Using this guide 25

The Route 27

Stage 1 – Test Valley . . . .
Winchester to Old Sarum 28
Stage 2 – Salisbury Plain . . . .
Old Sarum to Chirton 34
Stage 3 – Vale of Pewsey and Ridgeway Part I . . . .
Chirton to Uffington Castle 40
Stage 4 – Ridgeway Part II and Thames Valley . . . .
Uffington Castle to Reading 48
Stage 5 – Forest of Eversley . . . .
Reading to Farnham 54
Stage 6 – North Downs . . . .
Farnham to Forty Acre Lane 64
Stage 7 – South Downs . . . .
Forty Acre Lane to Winchester 73

Appendix A   Accommodation 82
Appendix B   Bike shops 88
Appendix C   Recommended kit lists 90

Bikepacking King Alfred's Way

Symbols used on route maps

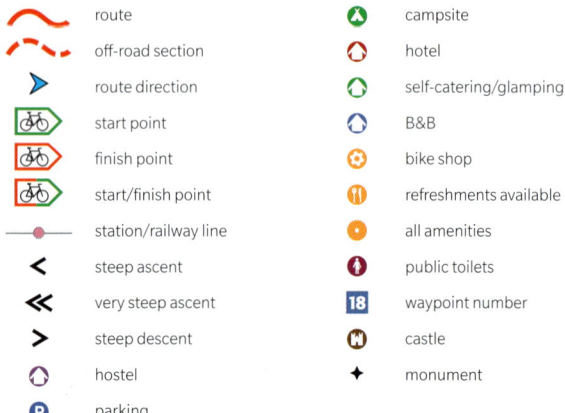

route	campsite
off-road section	hotel
route direction	self-catering/glamping
start point	B&B
finish point	bike shop
start/finish point	refreshments available
station/railway line	all amenities
steep ascent	public toilets
very steep ascent	waypoint number
steep descent	castle
hostel	monument
parking	

SCALE: 1:150,000

Contour lines are drawn at 50m intervals and labelled at 100m intervals. Route maps are drawn at 1:150,000 (1cm = 1.5km)

GPX files for all routes can be downloaded free at www.cicerone.co.uk/1238/GPX.

Features on the overview map

stage numbers	railway and station
alternative start point	

Fantastic fun on the wooded singletrack west of Tilshead (Stage 2)

Route summary table

	Stage	Start/Finish	Time	Total distance
1	Test Valley	Westgate, Winchester/Old Sarum, Salisbury	2hr 30min–3hr	40.1km (24.9 miles)
2	Salisbury Plain	Old Sarum/Chirton	4–5hr	49.5km (30.7 miles)
3	Vale of Pewsey and Ridgeway Part I	Chirton/Uffington Castle	4–6hr	51.7km (32.1 miles)
4	Ridgeway Part II and Thames Valley	Uffington Castle/Reading Station (near)	5–6hr	48.8km (30.1 miles)
5	Forest of Eversley	Reading Station (near)/Farnham	4–6hr	52.3km (32.5 miles)
6	North Downs	Farnham/Forty Acre Lane	6–7hr	59.4km (36.9 miles)
7	South Downs	Forty Acre Lane/King Alfred Statue, Winchester	4hr 30min–6hr	51.2km (31.8 miles)
Totals				353km (219 miles)

Acknowledgements

As well as thanking all the warm and helpful people I met along the route, I would like to give a huge thanks to the bikepackers who helped me research this guidebook: my partner, Nicky Stoupe; Kieron Chiswick; Norman Poole; Noah Harris; Duncan Parks; Clare Piconne; and Luke Morris.

MOD land criss-crossed with tank-friendly gravel tracks (Stage 2)

Route summary table

Off-road distance	% off-road	Ascent/ Descent	Grade	Way type (singletrack, track, road)	Page
20km	50%	470m/450m	🟩 / Easy	7%, 43%, 50%	28
35km	71%	500m/470m	🟩 / Easy	26%, 45%, 29%	34
39.5km	77%	670m/540m	🔺 / Moderate	14%, 63%, 23%	40
39.2km	81%	360m/560m	🔺 / Moderate	20%, 61%, 19%	48
24.7km	46%	360m/350m	🟩 / Easy	9%, 37%, 54%	54
37.9km	64%	700m/660m	🔺 / Moderate	20%, 44%, 36%	64
37km	74%	740m/790m	🔺 / Moderate	41%, 33%, 26%	72
		3800/3820m			

Safety and emergencies

Carry a charged mobile phone and backup power source(s). In case of serious injury, call 999 with your location (grid reference or What Three Words) and phone number. Bring a spare head torch, and ensure your sleeping bag suits the overnight temperature. Don't rely solely on one phone; it can easily become a single source of failure.

Bikepacking King Alfred's Way

Alternative schedules: wild camping

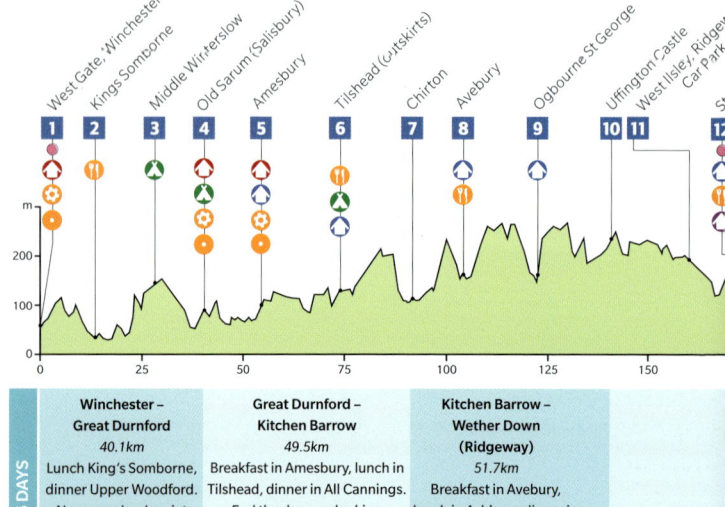

6 DAYS	**Winchester – Great Durnford** *40.1km* Lunch King's Somborne, dinner Upper Woodford. No access land; quiet spots can be found via Sarsen Way/Pewsey and Avon Trail	**Great Durnford – Kitchen Barrow** *49.5km* Breakfast in Amesbury, lunch in Tilshead, dinner in All Cannings. End the day overlooking the Vale of Pewsey	**Kitchen Barrow – Wether Down (Ridgeway)** *51.7km* Breakfast in Avebury, lunch in Ashbury, dinner in Letcombe Regis. End the day south of the Ridgeway
5 DAYS	**Winchester – Copehill Down / White Barrow** *72.8km* Lunch in Amesbury. Dinner in Tilshead. Camp below Tilshead	**Copehill Down / White Barrow – Segsbury Camp** *68.5km* Breakfast in Market Lavington, lunch in Ashbury, dinner in Letcombe Regis. Camp near the Ridgeway	
4 DAYS	**Winchester – Urchfont Hill** *89.6km* Lunch in Amesbury. Dinner in Market Lavington. Camp on Urchfont Hill	**Urchfont Hill – Streatley Warren** *85.2km* Breakfast in Avebury, lunch in Ashbury, dinner in East Ilsley. Camp on Streatley Warren	
3 DAYS	**Winchester – Overton Down** *122.3km* Lunch in Amesbury. Dinner in Avebury. Camp on Overton Down	**Overton Down – Bricksbury** *120.1km* Bring snacks for breakfast. Lunch in Reading, dinner in shot. Camp below Bricksbury	

Alternative schedules: wild camping

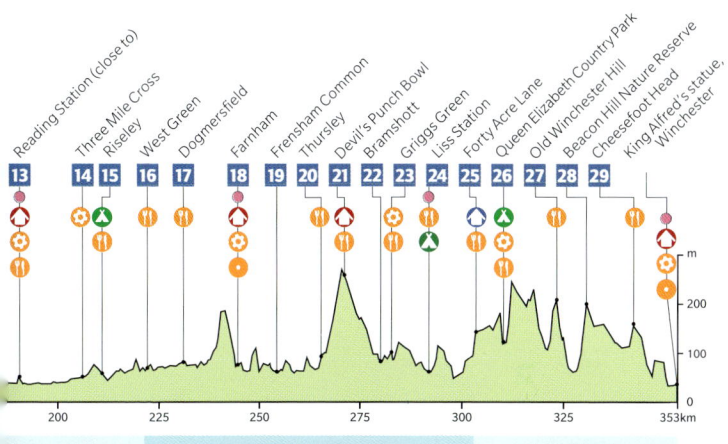

Wether Down – Hazeley Heath	Hazeley Heath – Durford Heath	Durford Heath – King Alfred Statue
79.2km	81.3km	51.2km
eakfast in East Ilsley, lunch in Reading, dinner in Hazeley. mp on Hazeley Heath	Breakfast in Hook, lunch at Devil's Punchbowl, dinner in Liss. Camp on Durford Heath	Breakfast at Durleigh Marsh Farm Shop. Lunch in Exton

egsbury Camp – Hazeley Heath	Hazeley Heath – Hen Wood	Hen Wood – King Alfred Statue
79.2km	92.5km	40km
fast in East Ilsley, lunch ding, dinner at The Mut- amp on Hazeley Heath	Breakfast in Hartley Wintney/Hook, lunch at Devil's Punchbowl, dinner in East Meon. Camp in Hen Wood	Breakfast in Exton. Lunch at Cheesefoot Head snack van

Streatley Warren – Thursley Common	Thursley Common – King Alfred Statue
89.9km	88.3km
Breakfast in Streatley, lunch in Reading, nner in Thursley. Camp on Thursley Common	Breakfast at Devil's Punchbowl visitor centre. Lunch at Queen Elizabeth visitor centre

Bricksbury Hill – King Alfred Statue
110.6km
Breakfast in Farnham. Lunch at Queen Elizabeth visitor centre

Distances are to the Waypoint number – actual camp spots may be further

Bikepacking King Alfred's Way

Alternative schedules: campsites

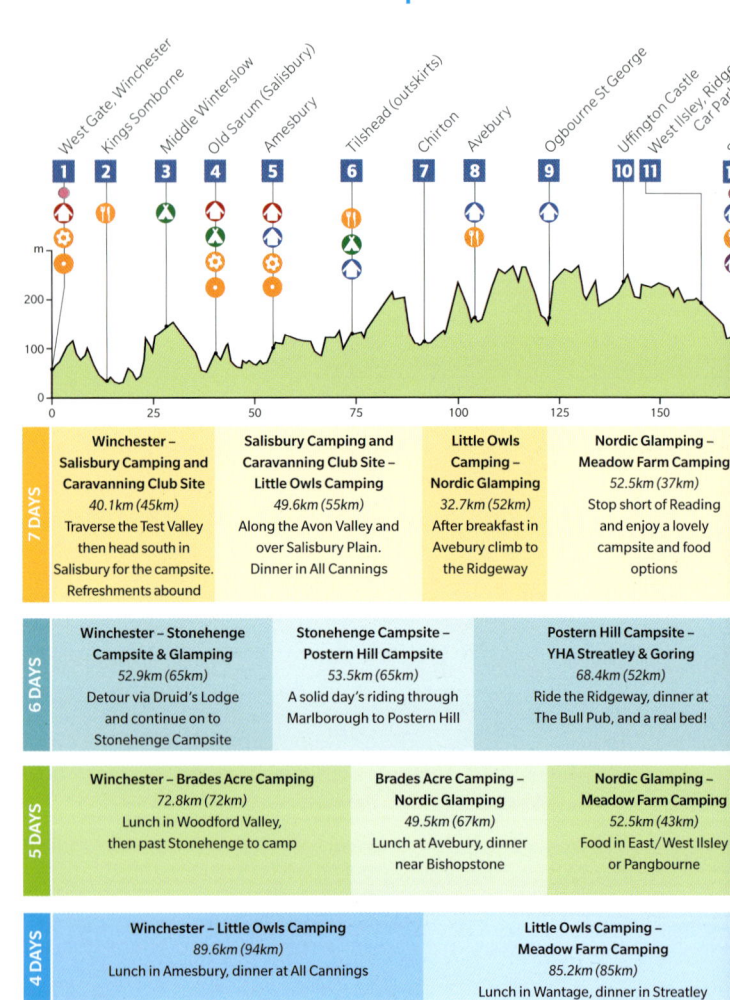

| 7 DAYS | Winchester – Salisbury Camping and Caravanning Club Site 40.1km (45km) Traverse the Test Valley then head south in Salisbury for the campsite. Refreshments abound | Salisbury Camping and Caravanning Club Site – Little Owls Camping 49.6km (55km) Along the Avon Valley and over Salisbury Plain. Dinner in All Cannings | Little Owls Camping – Nordic Glamping 32.7km (52km) After breakfast in Avebury climb to the Ridgeway | Nordic Glamping – Meadow Farm Camping 52.5km (37km) Stop short of Reading and enjoy a lovely campsite and food options |

| 6 DAYS | Winchester – Stonehenge Campsite & Glamping 52.9km (65km) Detour via Druid's Lodge and continue on to Stonehenge Campsite | Stonehenge Campsite – Postern Hill Campsite 53.5km (65km) A solid day's riding through Marlborough to Postern Hill | Postern Hill Campsite – YHA Streatley & Goring 68.4km (52km) Ride the Ridgeway, dinner at The Bull Pub, and a real bed! |

| 5 DAYS | Winchester – Brades Acre Camping 72.8km (72km) Lunch in Woodford Valley, then past Stonehenge to camp | Brades Acre Camping – Nordic Glamping 49.5km (67km) Lunch at Avebury, dinner near Bishopstone | Nordic Glamping – Meadow Farm Camping 52.5km (43km) Food in East/West Ilsley or Pangbourne |

| 4 DAYS | Winchester – Little Owls Camping 89.6km (94km) Lunch in Amesbury, dinner at All Cannings | Little Owls Camping – Meadow Farm Camping 85.2km (85km) Lunch in Wantage, dinner in Streatley |

Alternative schedules: campsites

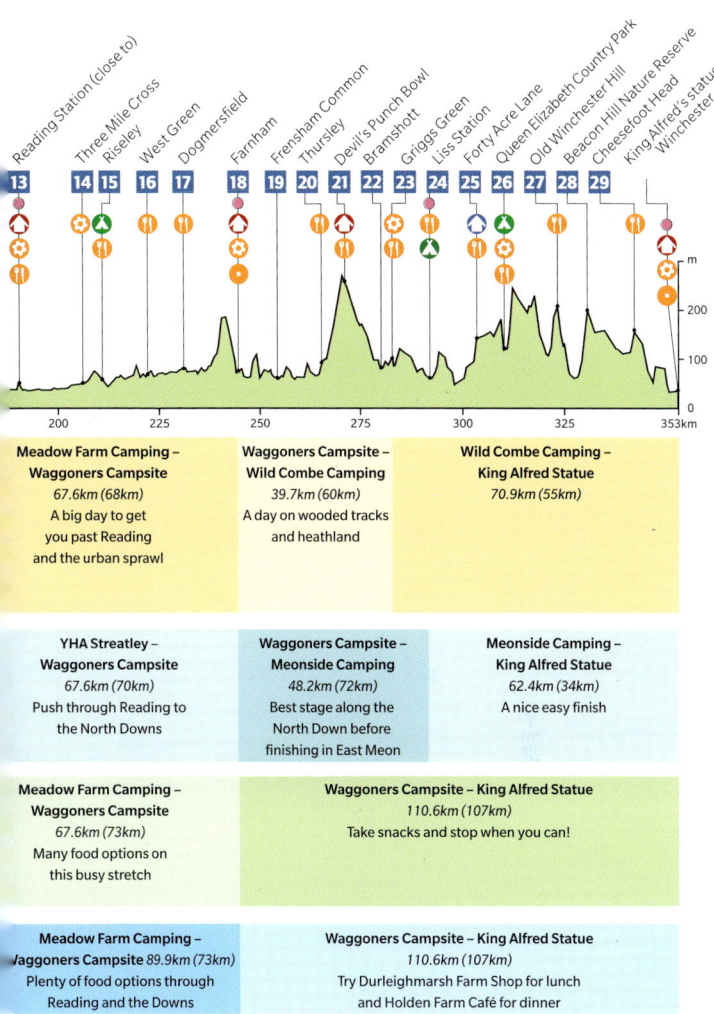

Meadow Farm Camping – Waggoners Campsite 67.6km (68km) A big day to get you past Reading and the urban sprawl	Waggoners Campsite – Wild Combe Camping 39.7km (60km) A day on wooded tracks and heathland	Wild Combe Camping – King Alfred Statue 70.9km (55km)
YHA Streatley – Waggoners Campsite 67.6km (70km) Push through Reading to the North Downs	Waggoners Campsite – Meonside Camping 48.2km (72km) Best stage along the North Down before finishing in East Meon	Meonside Camping – King Alfred Statue 62.4km (34km) A nice easy finish
Meadow Farm Camping – Waggoners Campsite 67.6km (73km) Many food options on this busy stretch	Waggoners Campsite – King Alfred Statue 110.6km (107km) Take snacks and stop when you can!	
Meadow Farm Camping – Waggoners Campsite 89.9km (73km) Plenty of food options through Reading and the Downs	Waggoners Campsite – King Alfred Statue 110.6km (107km) Try Durleighmarsh Farm Shop for lunch and Holden Farm Café for dinner	

Distances are to the Waypoint number, with distance to accommodation included (in brackets)

Alternative schedules: hostels and B&Bs

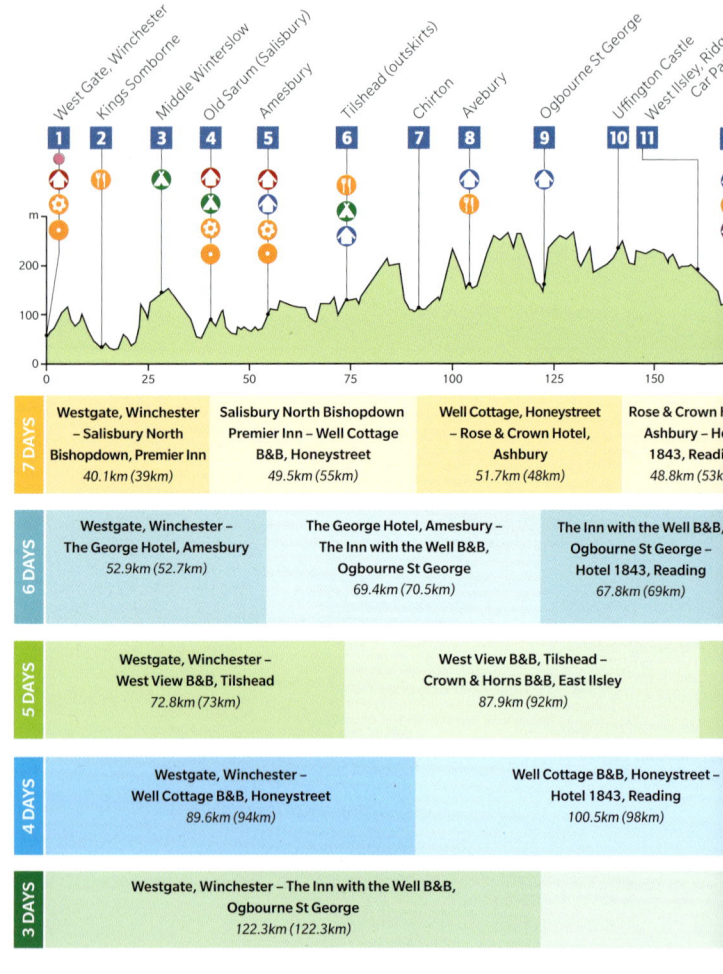

7 DAYS	Westgate, Winchester – Salisbury North Bishopdown, Premier Inn *40.1km (39km)*	Salisbury North Bishopdown Premier Inn – Well Cottage B&B, Honeystreet *49.5km (55km)*	Well Cottage, Honeystreet – Rose & Crown Hotel, Ashbury *51.7km (48km)*	Rose & Crown H Ashbury – Ho 1843, Readi *48.8km (53k*
6 DAYS	Westgate, Winchester – The George Hotel, Amesbury *52.9km (52.7km)*	The George Hotel, Amesbury – The Inn with the Well B&B, Ogbourne St George *69.4km (70.5km)*	The Inn with the Well B&B, Ogbourne St George – Hotel 1843, Reading *67.8km (69km)*
5 DAYS	Westgate, Winchester – West View B&B, Tilshead *72.8km (73km)*	West View B&B, Tilshead – Crown & Horns B&B, East Ilsley *87.9km (92km)*
4 DAYS	Westgate, Winchester – Well Cottage B&B, Honeystreet *89.6km (94km)*	Well Cottage B&B, Honeystreet – Hotel 1843, Reading *100.5km (98km)*
3 DAYS	Westgate, Winchester – The Inn with the Well B&B, Ogbourne St George *122.3km (122.3km)*

Alternative schedules: hostels and B&Bs

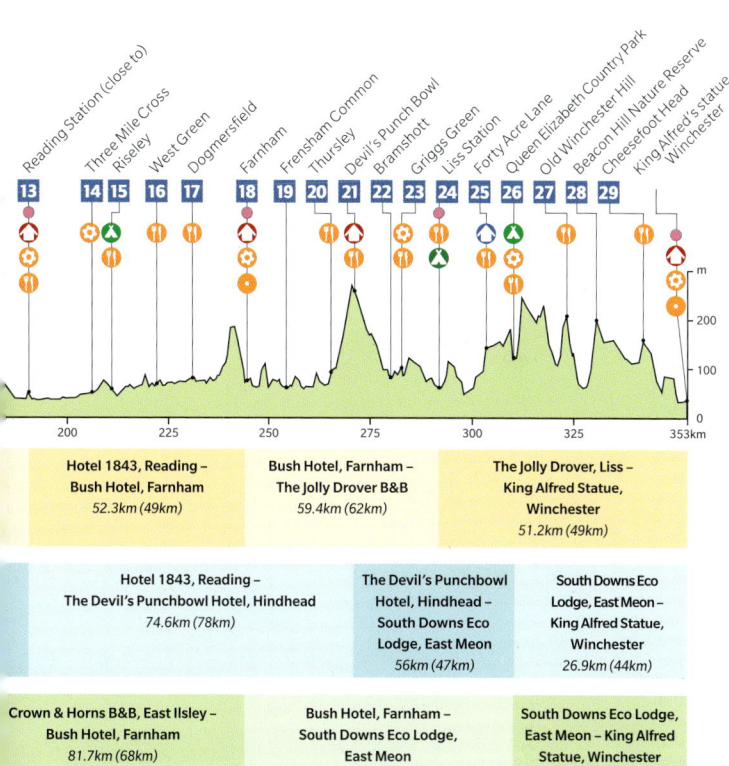

| Hotel 1843, Reading – Bush Hotel, Farnham 52.3km (49km) | Bush Hotel, Farnham – The Jolly Drover B&B 59.4km (62km) | The Jolly Drover, Liss – King Alfred Statue, Winchester 51.2km (49km) |

| Hotel 1843, Reading – The Devil's Punchbowl Hotel, Hindhead 74.6km (78km) | The Devil's Punchbowl Hotel, Hindhead – South Downs Eco Lodge, East Meon 56km (47km) | South Downs Eco Lodge, East Meon – King Alfred Statue, Winchester 26.9km (44km) |

| Crown & Horns B&B, East Ilsley – Bush Hotel, Farnham 81.7km (68km) | Bush Hotel, Farnham – South Downs Eco Lodge, East Meon 83.7km (76km) | South Downs Eco Lodge, East Meon – King Alfred Statue, Winchester 26.9km (44km) |

| Hotel 1843, Reading – The Jolly Drover, Liss 111.7km (93km) | The Jolly Drover, Liss – King Alfred Statue, Winchester 51.2km (69km) |

| The Inn with the Well B&B, Ogbourne St George – The Devil's Punchbowl Hotel, Hindhead 147.8km (147.8km) | The Devil's Punchbowl Hotel, Hindhead – King Alfred Statue, Winchester 82.9km (82.9km) |

Distances are to the Waypoint number, with distance to accommodation included (in brackets)

Climbing on a rough track east of Devenish nature reserve (Stage 2; photo Noah Harris)

Introduction

Descending to Keeper's Cottage (Stage 2)

Early in 2020, my mother forwarded me an article from *The Guardian* that had caught her eye. Cycling UK, Britain's leading cycling charity and advocacy group, was launching a new bikepacking route in southern England. The route promised to take riders through ancient landscapes, far from urban sprawl, motorways and traffic, guiding them through the power centres of Anglo-Saxon Wessex and taking them further back still to pre-Christian civilisations and the rites of the Druids. I was instantly hooked. I pitched the plan to two fellow bikepackers and a month later we were on the platform at 6am at London Blackfriars, ready to begin our journey.

It proved unforgettable. With perfect weather, we enjoyed blue skies and vast horizons, and we had much of the trail to ourselves. We crossed barrows, rode past castles, traversed chalk uplands and marvelled at Neolithic stone circles. We wild camped under the stars near Avebury the first night and stayed at a campsite near Reading the second. The memories of that ride will stay with me forever. Since then, I've returned to the route on four occasions, and I hope this familiarity comes through in the guide.

Bikepacking King Alfred's Way

A megalith at Avebury, the largest stone circle in the world (Stage 3; photo Noah Harris)

Created with Cycling UK, this guide will help you plan your own adventure. It includes 3–7-day schedules for all riding styles, options to tackle the route in sections, background history and all the logistics required to make your King Alfred's Way trip unforgettable.

What is bikepacking?

Bikepacking, like backpacking, involves setting out on a multi-day

Planning your ride

journey on which you'll need to carry the essentials required for your comfort when not riding (see Appendix C). If you're camping, you'll need at least a tent or bivvy bag, a sleeping bag, some food and possibly a means to prepare it.

What sets bikepacking apart from classic cycle touring is the terrain; instead of paved roads, you'll travel along bridleways, green lanes, forest tracks and forgotten rights of way. Sometimes, taking the road, or staying in a B&B or hostel, makes sense, but bikepacking is generally defined as an off-road cycling and camping adventure.

It also differs from traditional mountain biking: you won't find endless high-speed, technical descents here, although there are some, but instead a journey of exploration. Immersing yourself in ancient landscapes and remote trails becomes a kind of pilgrimage. This route is demanding, but it offers you a chance to undertake a remarkable, soul-stirring adventure that will stay with you long after the ride ends.

Planning your ride

Getting there

The route officially begins and ends in Winchester, in Southern England, and is served by South Western Railway and other operators. However, with many mainline stations nearby, such as Salisbury, Swindon, Reading, Guildford and Petersfield, you can easily start or finish at different points. This flexibility allows you to tailor the ride to your group's schedule, break it into weekend-friendly sections or adapt it to suit weather and time constraints. Many riders complete the route over multiple visits. Just be aware that some stations lie on different lines, which may require separate tickets or involve replacement buses. Always check your return options in advance and book bike spaces if required by your train operator.

When to go

There are a few factors to consider here. Typically, it's advisable to avoid riding this route in winter. Not necessarily because of the lower temperatures (it's easy enough to mitigate this with the right kit), but for the going. It's best to avoid the route after a period of wet weather because many of the tracks will be churned up and very muddy – and you don't want to contribute to this. Spring is a good time for the ride and so is autumn. The middle of summer is also going to be glorious, but this popular route could be busy and you may be sharing popular sections with walkers, horse riders, picnickers and dog walkers.

Choosing a schedule

This guide slices the route up into seven stages that make logical sense in terms of distance, each being close to 50km, and landscape, each being a different valley, section of upland or distinct habitat. However, your own preferences might well prompt a different approach. For example, if you are keen campers you may want to avoid ending a day's riding in Reading as there are few viable camping options. The Alternative Schedules are provided to cater for different styles of riding, and are intended as a guide – it is up to you to use your own judgement as to what is suitable for your group, both in advance and on the day. For instance, to make these schedules shorter, you could consider taking the train from Reading to Farnham, which saves half a day's riding and misses out on some ugly urban sprawl and gyratories!

There are three sets of Alternative Schedules: wild camping, campsites, and hostels and B&Bs. The wild camping schedules are for solo riders and very small groups, and include possible refreshment stops if you're not carrying your own food. Wild camping is a subjective, esoteric style of riding, and suggested sites are located within the waypoints provided, generally off-route. As such, the distances provided in the schedules are to the waypoint, so actual distances to your chosen wild-camp spot may be further. (Note that all wild camping choices are the responsibility of the rider – see 'Wild Camping' box for more). The campsite and hostel/B&B schedules include waypoint distances, with exact distances to the recommended accommodation listed (in brackets).

Route challenges

Individual stages of this route could definitely be classed as beginner friendly: the Test Valley and Salisbury Plain; even the Ridgeway stages are easy and straightforward in their own right. The final two stages – the North Downs and the South Downs – are the most technical and lumpy. One of the main challenges for a beginner might be the lack of obvious refreshment stops outside of the large towns; these will often require a detour so make sure you don't get caught out. Water is easier to find, especially if you can take water from streams and filter, boil or purify it.

Groups of riders

This route passes through a beautiful living landscape shaped by generations of farming and rural life. Many of the tracks run through working farms, and riders need to remember they are guests in a setting where people live and work. Please respect landowners, livestock and crops, and avoid disturbing the peace of the countryside.

While not wanting to be overly prescriptive, it's important to consider your impact and keep group sizes sensible (2–4 is ideal) out of respect for other users and to reduce wear on paths. Ride courteously: slow down for walkers, horses and children, and use a bell where appropriate. Enjoy the fast gravel and descents, but take time to stop, soak in the views and honour the heritage of this exceptional landscape.

What to take

Seventy per cent of this route is off-road and often hilly, and you'll be hauling your gear over rough terrain. Consider the conditions, pack light and allow for a margin of error based on the weather forecast. Choose the lightest gear that suits the conditions: don't bring a summer bag if it's going to be -1°C or a tarp if heavy rain is expected. The lighter your load, the more comfortable your ride. Evaluate each item for necessity and opt for tried-and-tested gear that serves multiple purposes. As an alternative you could skip the camping (and all the associated kit! – see Appendix C) altogether and stay in B&Bs or hotels.

Choice of bike

This route can be comfortably ridden on either a gravel bike or a mountain bike, although each comes with its own set of advantages and compromises. On a mountain bike, you might occasionally feel slowed down by the heavy tread of wider tyres, especially on smoother ground, but you'll likely be grateful for the extra grip and control when tackling steep, off-road climbs. Conversely, if you're on a gravel bike, you'll find yourself flying between villages on narrow country lanes, feeling confident in your choice, at least until the terrain turns rough.

A well-equipped gravel bike, ideally with a suspension stem or seat post and some knobbly tyres and a wide gear ratio, strikes a good balance for the variety of surfaces you'll encounter. That said, a mountain bike can also be adapted for the job: fitting it with narrower tyres and locking out

Dawn after a wild camp near East Meon (Stage 7)

Bikepacking King Alfred's Way

The Ridgeway is intersected by byways and bridleways (Stage 3)

the suspension makes for a surprisingly capable and comfortable set-up over longer distances.

The key is to avoid the extremes. A full-suspension mountain bike may limit your ability to carry luggage efficiently. At the other end of the spectrum, a gravel bike built more like a randonneur, with narrow 30–35mm tyres, could leave you feeling battered after 350km of mixed terrain. Technically, the route is rideable on a hybrid, but it's not something I'd recommend.

Whatever bike you take, ensure it's been serviced recently and that you have the tools and knowledge to make basic repairs. Make sure you take enough inner tubes, lights and any other replacement parts you might need. Bike shops in the area are listed in Appendix B at the back of the guide.

Rights of way

Riders are permitted to use bridleways, cycleways, green lanes and permissive bridleways. You are not permitted to ride on footpaths.

National Cycle Network

This network of routes, managed by Sustrans, is a wonderful resource. The routes in this guide often take advantage of the network when linking up sections of off-road cycling. They can be guaranteed to be relatively quiet and often picturesque.

Navigation

While a GPS device is helpful, don't rely solely on one; units can fail, especially in cold weather (keep them warm in a pocket if needed), and phones can run out of battery, so carry a power bank or two! Consider carrying a paper map and compass as backup.

Accommodation

Camping

This long-distance bikepacking route is best experienced by camping, with some sections offering ideal spots while others have fewer obvious opportunities. Appendix A lists campsites in clockwise order from Winchester, and some are noted within the directions. Most sites are open from Easter to September and booking ahead is recommended. Some campsites are also near excellent food options.

Wild camping

Defined as camping anywhere that isn't a licensed campsite, wild camping provides you with many great options. Although technically illegal in much of England, it is widely tolerated, providing you adhere to the following rules and guidelines:

- Where feasible, ask the landowner for permission to camp.
- Camp high and away from settlements. Where possible, head uphill, away from paths and buildings.
- Respect the privacy of others.
- Do not interfere with livestock.
- Camp late and leave early. As the day's ride comes to an end, keep an eye out for good spots so that you can identify a suitable camp spot before running out of light. In the morning, pack up your tent or bivvy before breakfast and get back on the road straight afterwards.
- Only wild camp solo or in small groups to avoid disturbing the environment and your neighbours.
- Bury human waste at least 25cm (10in) deep with your shovel. Do not pollute any water courses. Take toilet paper and wipes home.
- Leave no trace. Take any litter home.

Bikepacking King Alfred's Way

Wild camping on King Alfred's Way

When wild camping on King Alfred's Way, choose your pitch carefully, ideally on common land (marked by a tan border on 1:25 OS® maps), near intersecting bridleways for easy access. Additionally, support Trash Free Trails, an organisation dedicated to keeping UK trails free of plastic pollution. For more info, visit facebook.com/trashfreetrails.

Other accommodation options

Unusually for a bikepacking guide, a limited number of B&Bs, hotels and YHAs are included, which could be worth considering if you fancy a bed for the night. These are marked on the maps and schedules, and their details are listed in Appendix A.

Fuel strategies

Bikepacking is physically demanding, especially off road for multiple days. Consider how self-supporting you and your group will be. Ensure everyone agrees on food expectations or acknowledges differences before starting. Sometimes, choices may be limited.

Bring your own food

Weight and packability are crucial. Avoid cooking complex meals, such as fried breakfasts or stews. Opt for

Preparing lunch on Beacon Hill (Stage 7)

foods that don't require heating, such as oatcakes, cheese, chorizo and fruit. If you prefer hot food, consider boil-in-the-bag meals, canned beans or dehydrated foods. Dehydrated meals are lightweight, have a long shelf life and require only boiling water and some insulation (like a sleeping bag) to rehydrate. You can prepare these yourself or buy from speciality suppliers.

Rely on local infrastructure
A pub lunch can be a great treat. Alternatively, plan a visit to a shop near the end of your ride to pick up supplies and lighten your load (a micro rucksack is useful). You can also arrive at a pub before they stop serving, enjoy dinner and then bivvy under the stars.

Hybrid model
Mix it up by bringing your own breakfast, such as overnight oats or granola with milk powder, and a few portions of dehydrated food as a backup. Take advantage of opportunities to visit excellent country inns throughout the area.

Snacks
Dried fruit, nuts, cereal bars and protein bars are commercially available or can be made in advance.

Hydration
The importance of keeping hydrated cannot be understated. Take any opportunity to refill your water bottles. There is no need to carry large quantities of water with you as you can refill from countless streams. You can filter the water; Sawyer is a brand to look out for. Consider adding electrolyte powder to improve hydration but remember to keep some water free of flavouring if you plan to use it to make coffee or hydrate food!

About the route

Cycling UK and King Alfred's Way
Launched by Cycling UK (formerly the CTC, founded in 1878) in 2020, King Alfred's Way was the result of three years of collaboration with local councils and landowners. Designed to highlight the region's rich history and varied landscapes, the route weaves together major long-distance trails, such as the Ridgeway, South Downs Way, North Downs Way and Thames Path, with lesser-known routes, including the White Horse Trail, Monarch's Way, Sussex Border Path, Greensand Way, Shipwrights Way, Allan King Way, Itchen Way, Clarendon Way and Sarsen Way. Cycling UK also petitioned to upgrade footpaths to bridleways, enabling access for riders. The route traverses Berkshire, Wiltshire, Hampshire and Surrey and touches on Oxfordshire and West Sussex.

Prehistoric and Neolithic history
From its start at Westgate, Winchester, to its culmination at the statue of King Alfred the Great in the city centre,

In the spring the wild meadow flowers are in bloom (Stage 2)

your journey traces England's ancient history, linking Neolithic sites along pre-existing 'roads'. You pass Old Sarum, Salisbury's prehistoric hub, then Amesbury, near Stonehenge, and ride through Avebury, the world's largest stone circle. Along the White Horse Trail you encounter long barrows, Wayland's Smithy and ancient forts, including Barbury, Uffington, Liddington Castle and Segsbury Camp.

King Alfred the Great and Wessex

England's famous Anglo-Saxon sovereign, King Alfred the Great, established his power base in Wessex, a long-vanished kingdom that encompassed much of what is now Hampshire, Dorset, Wiltshire and Somerset. Born in 849CE at a royal estate near Wantage, Alfred became king in 871 and played a pivotal role in uniting the Anglo-Saxon kingdoms and defending them against Viking invasions. He is celebrated for his military victories, including the crucial Battle of Edington in 878, as well as his reforms in law, education and governance. Winchester was the capital of Wessex and Alfred's primary seat of power, which is why a prominent statue of him stands in the city today. Commissioned in 1899, it was erected in 1901 to mark the thousandth anniversary of the death of one of England's greatest monarchs.

Wildlife and working landscape

This route winds through the heart of rural England, crossing diverse habitats, including the chalk grasslands of the South Downs and Wiltshire Downs, home to butterflies like the Duke of Burgundy and Dark Green Fritillary, hares and muntjac deer. In the ancient woodlands of the North Wessex Downs and Surrey Hills, woodpeckers, owls and nuthatches thrive. Kingfishers frequent the chalk streams of the Test Valley, and, if you're lucky, you might spot a great bustard, reintroduced to Salisbury Plain. Along the way, working farms enrich the landscape, with arable fields of wheat, barley and oats giving way to grazing cattle and sheep, connecting riders to the deep heritage of this ancient land.

Using this guide

Approach this ride knowing your limits and decide when, or if, to push them. Consider the difficulty, timing, weather and route conditions. Use the route profile for guidance on when to refuel or rest. Plan accommodation in advance or be prepared to adjust on the go.

Three sample Alternative Schedules are offered: wild camping, campsites, and hostels and B&Bs. These schedules range from three to seven days, depending on your pace and daily distance.

Stage components

This guide for King Alfred's Way has the following components:

- **Information box**: the first place to look when accessing the upcoming stage. It provides the start/finish, time, distance, ascent/descent, grade (based on the hardest stage), terrain and percentage of off-road riding.

- **Introduction**: a brief description of the stage and its highlights.

- **Summary table**: key details of each numbered waypoint of the stage, including distance, ascent/descent, surface, grade and a description highlighting important aspects of the stage. The waypoints are logical blocks within a stage but are not necessarily equal in length – they correlate more closely to terrain or refuelling and rest options.

- **Turn-by-turn directions**: the main component of each route, which you can follow alongside the inline map if you need to rely on the guide rather than the GPX on a device. It's recommended that you read these detailed directions before setting off, so that you are aware in advance of any challenges ahead.

Direction arrows indicate left (←), right (→) and straight ahead (↑).

Difficulty grading

While this guide uses mountain bike (MTB) grades to suggest the technical difficulty of each off-road numbered waypoint, the stages as a whole have also been given an overall descriptive grade (easy, moderate, difficult) that takes the route's other qualities into account.

Off-road grades are based on British Cycling standards:

- **Green/Easy**: Flat, even ground with shallow climbs; suitable for most riders; no special skills needed.

- **Blue/Moderate**: Basic mountain biking skills required; includes minor obstacles, moderate gradients and occasional steep descents with semi-technical features.

Road waypoints have not been graded. Any difficult road sections can be identified through warnings in the guide and notes or chevrons (denoting steep gradients) on the map.

GPX tracks

Download GPX tracks for these routes at cicerone.co.uk/1238/GPX. If you purchased the book outside the Cicerone website or without an account, please register it via the 'My account' tab on the Cicerone website for access to GPX files and updates.

The GPX files are provided in a standard format compatible with most devices, but you may need to convert them using a tool such as gpsvisualizer.com. The author and publisher are not responsible for any issues arising from their use.

The Route

Approaching the Hartley Steps, a steep climb that will test your nerve (Stage 4)

1 — 50% off road

Stage 1 – Test Valley

Winchester to Old Sarum

Start/Finish	Westgate, Winchester/Old Sarum
Time	2hr 30min–3hr
Total distance	40.1km (24.9 miles)
Off-road distance	20km
Percentage off-road	50%
Total ascent/descent	470/450m
Grade	Easy ■
Terrain	Singletrack 7%, track 43%, road 50%

The opening stage is a mellow introduction. After a gentle climb out of Winchester, you head north-west into the rolling arable pastures south of Sparsholt before crossing the tranquil River Test as it intersects the chalk downlands. Your westward course takes you out of Hampshire into Wiltshire, along the course of the old Roman road that makes up part of the Monarch's Way: the long-distance footpath that plots the course of King Charles II after his defeat at the Battle of Worcester. After crossing the River Bourne, a tributary of the Avon, you head directly to the imposing earthwork ramparts of Old Sarum: the Iron Age hill fort considered Salisbury's prehistoric centre.

Summary table

Waypoint	Section	Distance	Ascent	Descent	Surface	Grade	Description
1	Westgate, Winchester – King's Somborne	13.6km	120m	150m	mixed	■	An easy climb out of Winchester but don't miss the concealed turn-off to the byway
2	King's Somborne – Middle Winterslow	14.3km	220m	120m	mixed	■	Nice views heading west; watch out for the byway turn-off in Middle Winterslow

Winchester to Old Sarum

Waypoint	Section	Distance	Ascent	Descent	Surface	Grade	Description
3	Middle Winterslow–Old Sarum (Salisbury)	12.2km	130m	180m	Mixed	■	Easy rolling directly west following the old Roman road

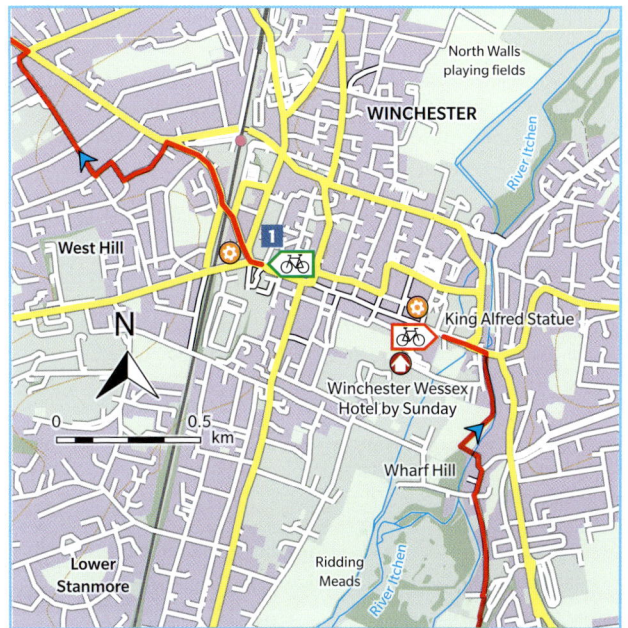

Directions

1 ■ The official route starts and finishes at different locations within ancient Winchester: Westgate and the statue of King Alfred the Great, respectively. With the cobbled street of the historic Westgate behind you, take the second exit on the mini roundabout, signposted 'All traffic routes, Station'. Climb Upper High Street, take a ← marked as a cycle route and cross over the **railway**. At the mini roundabout turn → onto St Paul's Hill. At the next mini roundabout go ←, signposted 'Sparsholt, Stockbridge, Salisbury', and then immediately ← onto Elm Road, followed by → onto Avenue Road then ← onto

Stage 1 – Test Valley

Western Road. Turn ➔ at the Fulflood Arms pub onto leafy Cheriton Road. Bear ➔ and at the mini roundabout, turn ← onto Stockbridge Road.

At the box junction 300m later, turn ← onto Dean Lane. After 1.5km a gravel layby marks the start of the off-road. You fork ← onto a narrow dirt single-track permissive byway. After 1km rejoin the road at Woodman Lane, turn ➔, after 100m fork ← onto Ham Green Lane. After 1km head through the yard of the red brick Moor Court Farm. Here the landscape opens up before you as the car-wide gravel drive snakes along the valley floor and woodland frames your view to the left and right. Rejoin the road at Forest Extra and continue on Chalk Vale. At the first junction, bear ← and at the second turn ➔ signed 'King's Somborne'. On meeting the Winchester Road, give way and then turn ←. Continue into **King's Somborne**.

2 ■ Climb gently through the town. Turn ➔ over the **chalk stream** and continue ← on Old Vicarage Lane before turning ←. When you reach the busy A3057, turn ← and then opposite the parish church, with the thatched Crown Inn pub on your right, bear ➔ (possible lunch spot depending on timings). After 800m fork ➔, signposted 'Horsebridge, Houghton'. In Horsebridge take a ➔ signed 'Houghton'. Cross the **River Test** and continue towards Houghton. After a series of bridges, you reach the village and turn ➔, 'Stockbridge, Houghton Lodge Gardens'. After 400m, by a small post box, turn ← onto

Studying the map at Westgate, Winchester

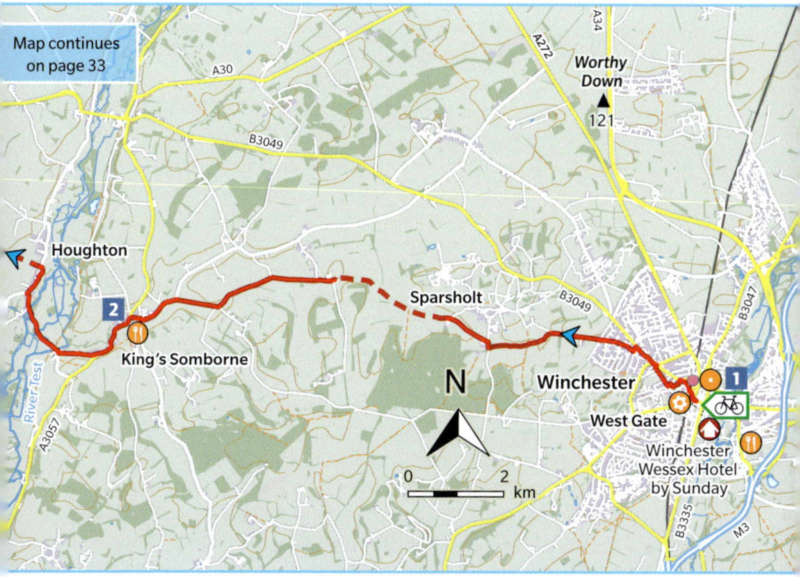

Winchester to Old Sarum

Map continues on page 33

The landscape opens up after Moor Court Farm

Stage 1 - Test Valley

Stevens Drove. When the asphalt runs out you join a byway. At the fork in 2km turn ←. When you meet the tarmac of Rookery Lane, turn →.

At the junction in **Broughton** turn → onto High street. At the Grey Hound pub, bear ← on Queenwood Road. At the green, turn → then immediately ← onto Buckholt Road, signed 'Monarch's Way, Clarendon Way'. After 200m fork → on a byway. Climb to Smith's Plantation then fork → once more. Continue ↑ for 2km. At Little Buckholt Farm bear ← before turning → and regaining the road. After 2.5km on an old Roman road, you reach **Middle Winterslow** on Easton Common Hill.

Beyond the Test, north of Salisbury

Winchester to Old Sarum

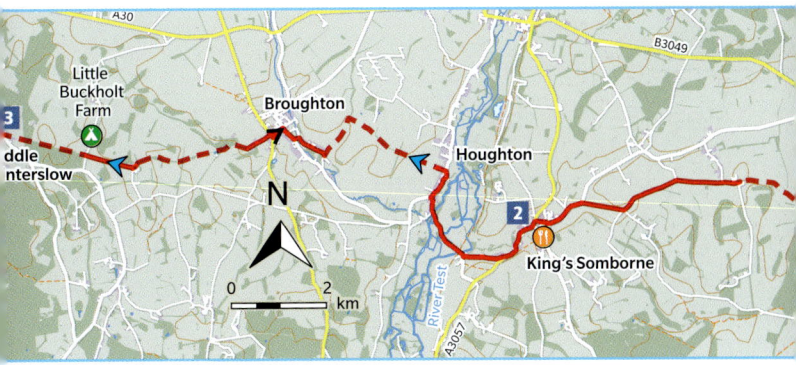

> The Monarch's Way is a 625-mile long-distance footpath that traces the escape route taken by King Charles II following his defeat by Cromwell in the Battle of Worcester in 1651. For six weeks, the 21-year-old king was hotly pursued by Parliamentarian troops but managed to evade capture and escape to France.

3 ■ At the road, turn ← and then immediately → at the junction, signed 'Winterslow, Salisbury'. When the road bears left, fork → onto a byway signed 'unsuitable for HGVs, The Flashett'. After 50m take the ← fork and then, after a further 50m, fork → past a detached red brick house. Continue on The Causeway, and when you meet Middleton Road, turn →. Climb gently and when the road bears left, fork → onto Roman Road. When this bears right, continue ↑ onto a byway, continuing on the course of the Monarch's Way, signed 'Cobb Lane'. As this descends to the left, take the → fork and continue to the road and turn →. At the crossroads take the ←, signed 'Pitton'. After 50m turn → as the Roman road continues on your right.

Continue on this for 3.5km, through a gate, across a road and into the next field on the byway. Head through the gate and join the **A30** road before forking → onto Old Malthouse Lane. After 10m turn → onto a bridleway and descend into the wood. After 1km continue under the **railway** before crossing the A338 onto Hurdcott Lane. A gentle climb takes you into the village and before the road bears right, fork ← onto a bridleway. Cross the River Bourne, climb for 50m then fork ←. Continue for 800m to the road and turn →. Back on the Roman road, continue to a junction, fork → onto Old Castle Road. Cross the A345 and take signs for the monument of **Old Sarum**. Old Sarum is known as the ancient heart of Salisbury and has Iron Age origins.

2 — 71% off road

Stage 2 – Salisbury Plain
Old Sarum to Chirton

Start/Finish	Old Sarum/Chirton
Time	4–5hr
Total distance	49.5km (30.7 miles)
Off-road distance	35km
Percentage off-road	71%
Total ascent/descent	500/470m
Grade	Easy ■
Terrain	Singletrack 26%, track 45%, road 29%

Heading north along the River Avon, this section passes through a selection of pretty rural villages to the historic town of Amesbury, one of the UK's oldest continuously inhabited settlements. From here you push west onto Salisbury Plain: a vast chalk plateau characterised by grasslands intermittently punctuated by trees and the occasional tank on manoeuvres. The ancient Neolithic monument Stonehenge dominates views to the south. The route continues north on minor roads and byways through the wide-open chalk downs to the White Horse Trail. Here you maintain the high ground of the Wessex Ridgeway before a spectacular singletrack down Chirton Bottom drops you to the Andover Road and the village of Chirton.

Summary table

Waypoint	Section	Distance	Ascent	Descent	Surface	Grade	Description
4	Old Sarum (Salisbury) – Amesbury	12.8km	150m	160m	mixed	■	Pub options off-route before Amesbury
5	Amesbury – Tilshead (outskirts)	19.9km	190m	140m	mixed	■	Keep a lookout for Stonehenge

Old Sarum to Chirton

Waypoint	Section	Distance	Ascent	Descent	Surface	Grade	Description
6	Tilshead (outskirts) – Chirton	16.8km	160m	170m	Mixed	■	Your first section of chalk upland

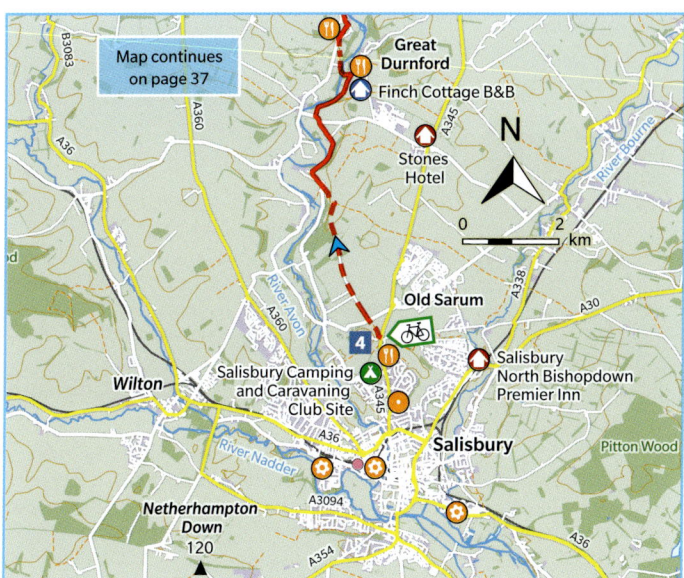

Directions

4 ■ To the left of double metal gates, below the mound, take a well-signed bridleway on the → for the Pewsey Avon Trail. The chalk singletrack drops you to a road; cross this and continue ↑ through a gate on a good, car-wide track. Maintain your direction for 2km before forking ← and descending to Salterton Farm. Bear → and follow Beech Walk through Netton.

After the phone box, continue for 100m, keeping an old stone wall behind you, and take the second →, signed 'Great Durnford'. This leafy lane follows the course of the river. Before you reach The Great Bustard pub (a possible pricey option for a lunch stop) in **Great Durnford**, take a wide gravel bridleway on your ←, marked 'Sarsen Way'. Head over a footbridge spanning the River Avon, turn → and climb across a field on a rough track to the road.

Stage 2 – Salisbury Plain

A good track leads you off Old Sarum

Turn ➔ and follow the road as it bears left, continuing through Wilsford and West Amesbury. When you meet Stonehenge Road (A303), turn ➔, signed 'Amesbury', and continue over the bridge and along Church Street then High Street into **Amesbury**.

5 ■ At the crossroads opposite the garage turn ←, signed 'Marlborough', and head up Countess Road. Use the cycleway on your right to cross the busy roundabout, following the sign for Pewsey, Upavon, Durrington and Lark Hill Garrison. Continue for 250m. Immediately after the entrance to a cul-de-sac, turn ← through a gate onto a bridleway. Bear ➔ and, unless taking the described detour to view Stonehenge, ignore the byway heading left and bear ← at the next fork, followed by a quick ← then ➔. When the track meets a T-junction, turn ➔. For better views of Stonehenge, turn ← onto the restricted byway past Halfmoon Clump to the Old King Barrows, which passes within 200m of Stonehenge – afterwards, retrace your track and rejoin the route.

> **Salisbury Plain**, a large chalk plateau characterised by open grassland, is home to dozens of significant archaeological sites, including, arguably, England's most famous landmark, Stonehenge. Constructed between

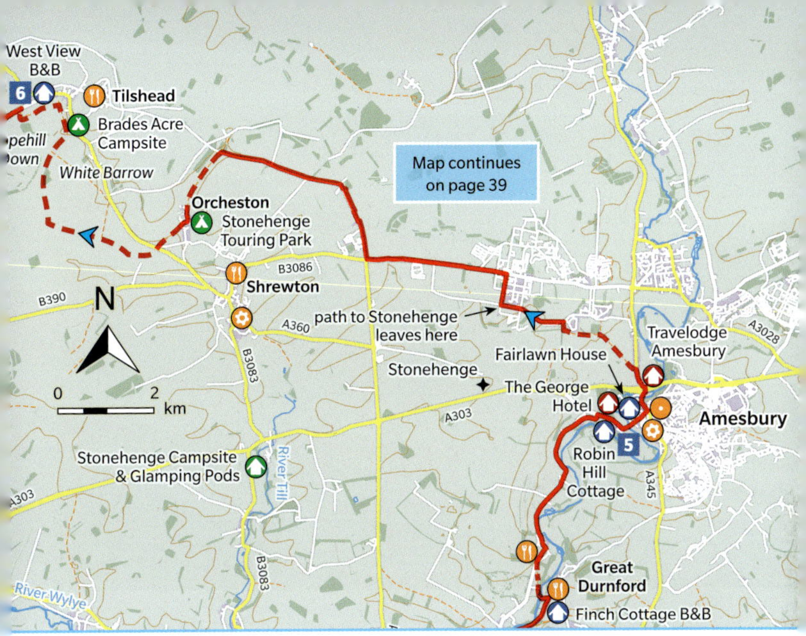

3000 and 1600BCE, the site consists of dozens of freestanding stones, some weighing around 25 tons. The stone circle was of great ceremonial significance over the course of two millennia, and today people still converge at the monument to celebrate the summer and winter solstices.

On meeting the road turn ← and continue to Larkhill Royal School of Artillery. Turn ← onto The Packway. After 1km turn →, signed 'Rollestone, MOD QinetiQ'. After 10m turn ← and take the bridleway as it runs adjacent to the road for 2km. At the next crossroads continue on the bridleway and turn →. After 1km, at Bustard Cottages, turn ← onto a byway running adjacent to the road.

Hug the edge of the wheat fields north of Shrewton

Stage 2 – Salisbury Plain

Dropping down to the Andover Road, near Chirton

After 2km turn ← onto a track running along the northern shoulder of Elston Hill. Unless stopping for the night, continue past the entrance to Stonehenge Touring Park and into **Orcheston**. The road bears left at the phone box but you turn → onto the restricted bridleway and climb the track to the road and turn →. Cross the A360 and continue on a car-wide track before turning → after 100m.

After 2km of exposed car-wide track, at the intersection of a second byway, turn → and ride uphill. After 1.5km follow the byway past a small chunk of common land by White Barrow, possibly a good place for a wild camp if it's getting late. Descend and then fork ← on the Imber Range Perimeter Path. Fork ← again and climb on the bridleway along the edge of a field before enjoying a fast section of singletrack through a wood. Continue to the road on the outskirts of **Tilshead** and turn ←. Refreshments and a campsite can be found in Tilshead.

6 ■ After 200m, turn → onto a bridleway. Continue north on the Imber Range Perimeter Path until you reach the road. Turn →, head through Gore Cross and up the hill on the White Horse Trail. With Market Lavington below to your left, continue on the Wessex Ridgeway for 5km around the shoulder of **Urchfont Hill**. If in need of refreshments, make a detour from the route to Market Lavington. At 800m beyond a small car park at the top of Redhorn Hill Road, turn ← onto a rough bridleway by Chirton Maggot. Descend for 1.5km

Old Sarum to Chirton

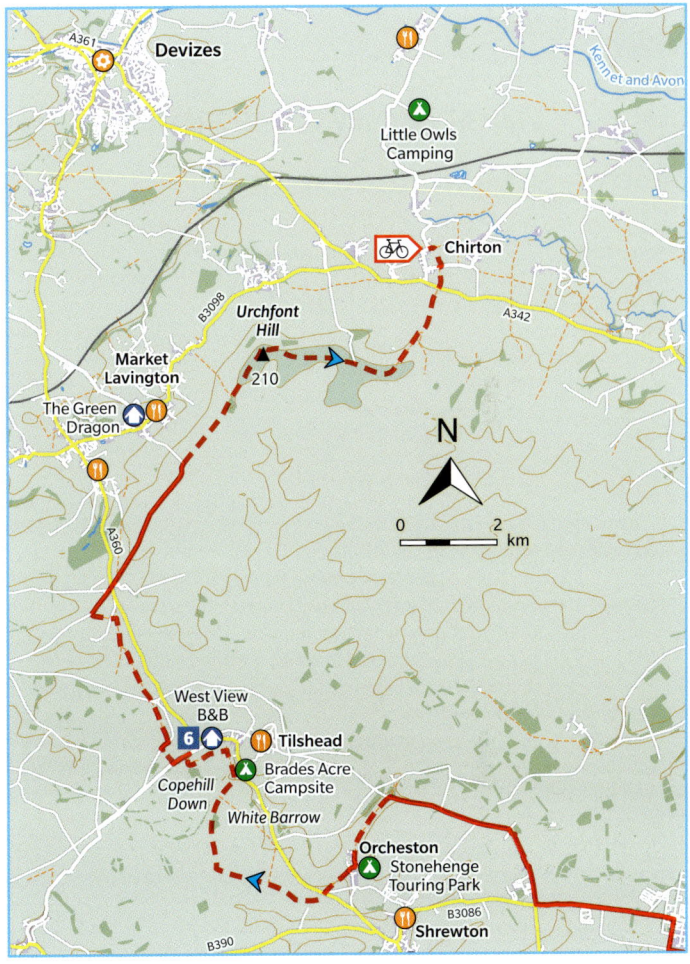

to the Andover Road. Cross the road and continue on a track running along the right of a line of trees to Small Street. Turn → then immediately ← onto a track. At the end of the track, turn ← and at the road, turn → and cross the northern bounds of **Chirton**.

3 77% off road

Stage 3 – Vale of Pewsey and Ridgeway Part I
Chirton to Uffington Castle

Start/Finish	Chirton/Uffington Castle
Time	4–6hr
Total distance	51.7km (32.1 miles)
Off-road distance	39.5km
Percentage off-road	77%
Total ascent/descent	670/540m
Grade	Moderate ▲
Terrain	Singletrack 14%, track 63%, road 23%

With Salisbury Plain behind you to the south, the Vale of Pewsey stretches out to the north towards the Marlborough Downs. Your route bisects the chalk uplands east of Kitchen Barrow and west of Clifford's Hill and the Pewsey White Horse Monument beyond. The descent into Avebury, home of the largest stone circle in the world, is unforgettable. From here you climb to join the Ridgeway, one of the oldest roads in Britain, and maintain this high ground to Barbury Castle before joining the Sarsen Way. After crossing the Og Valley and regaining the Ridgeway, you journey north, first passing the site of Liddington Castle to the west before journeying past Wayland's Smithy long barrow to the hill fort of Uffington Castle.

Summary table

Waypoint	Section	Distance	Ascent	Descent	Surface	Grade	Description
7	Chirton – Avebury	16.8km	180m	140m	mixed	▲	A tough climb before a wild descent
8	Avebury – Ogbourne St George	15.9km	190m	210m	off-road	▲	The Ridgeway proper; easy but can be rutted

Chirton to Uffington Castle

Waypoint	Section	Distance	Ascent	Descent	Surface	Grade	Description
9	Ogbourne St George – Uffington Castle	19km	300m	190m	off-road	▲	Fantastic views; refreshments below the ridge to the north

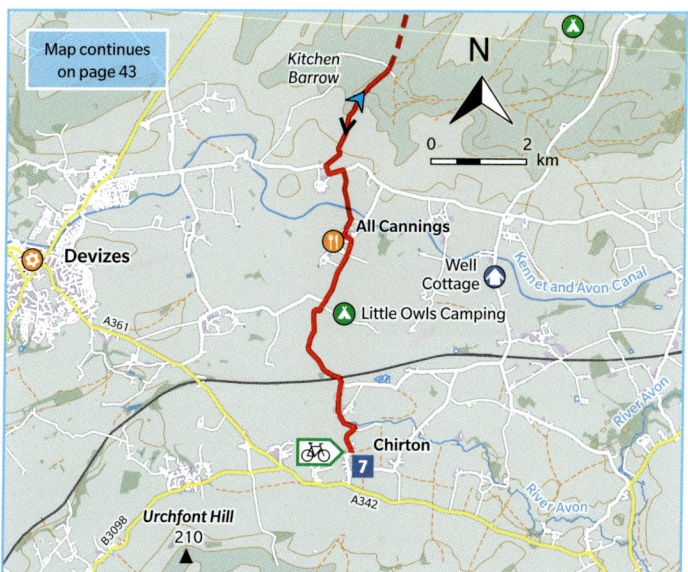

Directions

7 ▲ Follow the road through Patney, bear ← and cross over the **railway line**. Continue to All Cannings. Turn ← at the cemetery onto Chandlers Lane. At the junction turn → and then bear ← through the village. The Kings Arms in All Cannings is a great pub with excellent food options. After the green the asphalt runs out and you take a byway on the → across the fields towards Allington. At the road turn ←. The road bears left but you take a bridleway on the →, signed 'private road, bridleway only'. Climb steadily on a great car-wide track that takes a pass between two hills. The views are exceptional.

Now descend for 4km over Allington Down to the outskirts of Avebury. When the byway meets the road turn ← and then → at the A361. At the

The beginning of a spectacular climb east of Kitchen Barrow

roundabout take the second exit, signposted 'Avebury'. After 50m take a bridleway on your ←. After 100m turn → on the Wessex Ridgeway. Continue on South Street to the junction and turn ←. Follow the road as it bears ← and when it meets Bray Street, turn →. Continue on Church Walk as it bears →, and on to High Street. Continue into the stone circle that surrounds the village of **Avebury**.

8 ▲ At the junction, with the Red Lion pub on your left, continue for 100m. If you have time, it's worth stopping at the Red Lion, which offers a great selection of ales and passable food. As the road swings left, continue ↑ onto a minor road signed 'No visitor Parking Beyond this point'. When the asphalt runs out after 800m, continue your climb out onto the Wessex Ridgeway. The Ridgeway is known as England's first road. For more than 5000 years, this high chalk upland has provided travellers with a route between the south coast of Dorset and Norfolk in the east. When you reach the brow of the hill, where your track intersects with the Sarsen Way, turn ← onto NCN 45 and climb gently on a rutted track. After 4km cross a road and after a further 1.5km cross another road. Head through a metal gate and climb steeply, bearing → on the Sarsen Way/Ridgeway. The route takes you through the centre of the remains of **Barbury Castle** (toilet facilities can be found in the car park).

Chirton to Uffington Castle

Barbury Castle, an Iron Age hill fort, was first occupied 2500 years ago and remained in use into the Roman period. Originally, it would have had wooden fortifications. Today, only two defensive ditches remain. A short climb onto these provides exceptional views south across the Marlborough Downs.

Bear → as the car-wide track continues past Upper Herdswick Farm. Take the well-signposted gateway on your left and join the Ridgeway. Enjoy a unique descent over open ground along Smeathe's Ridge before gently climbing to the road. Turn → and when the road bears left to **Ogbourne St George**, continue ↑ onto the byway.

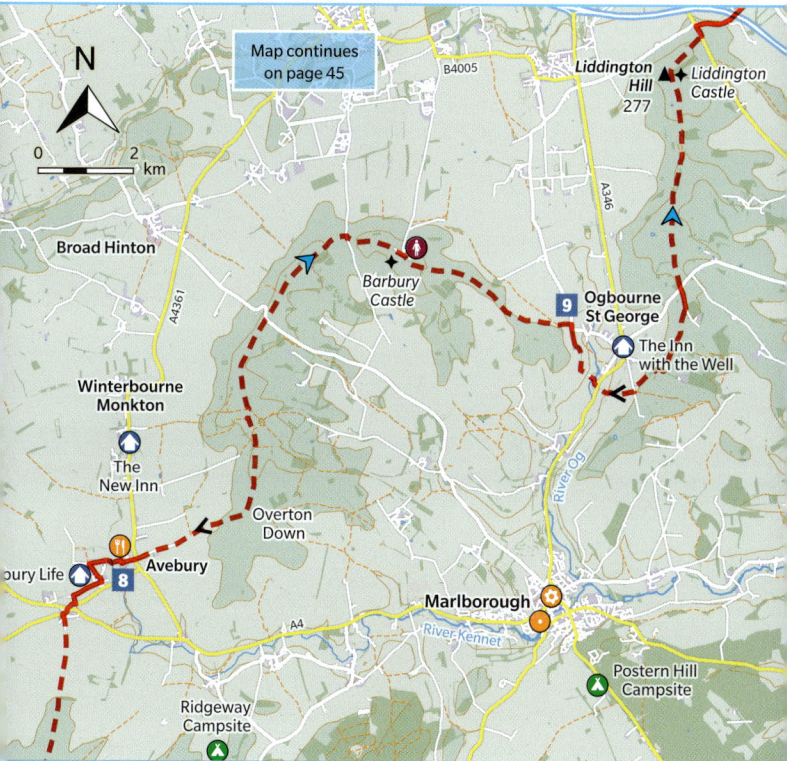

Stage 3 – Vale of Pewsey and Ridgeway Part I

9 ▲ After 1km, turn ← and descend to Southend. Cross the A346 and continue ↑ on the byway. Descend gently, cross NCN 482 as it runs along an old railway track and bear ← on the byway before climbing steeply. At the intersection of two byways bear → and then immediately turn ←, continuing on the Ridgeway for 6.5km, ignoring forks to the east and west.

Descend **Liddington Hill** to the gate and join the busy B4192. Turn ← and after 200m turn →, signposted 'Baydon, Bishopstone, Hinton Parva'. Follow this for 2km as it crosses first the M4 and then Callas Hill before delivering you back to the trail at Foxhill, where you turn → and climb steeply on a rough track onto the Ridgeway once more. For obvious reasons the Ridgeway itself has few refreshment stops and you will have to leave the route if you need to refuel. Both Bishopstone and Ashbury have fantastic country pubs. Numerous byways and roads intersect your route

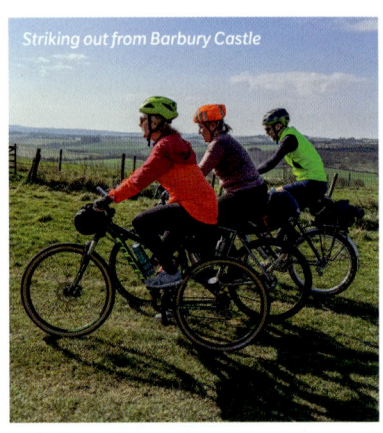
Striking out from Barbury Castle

There is an eerie atmosphere at Wayland's Smithy

Chirton to Uffington Castle

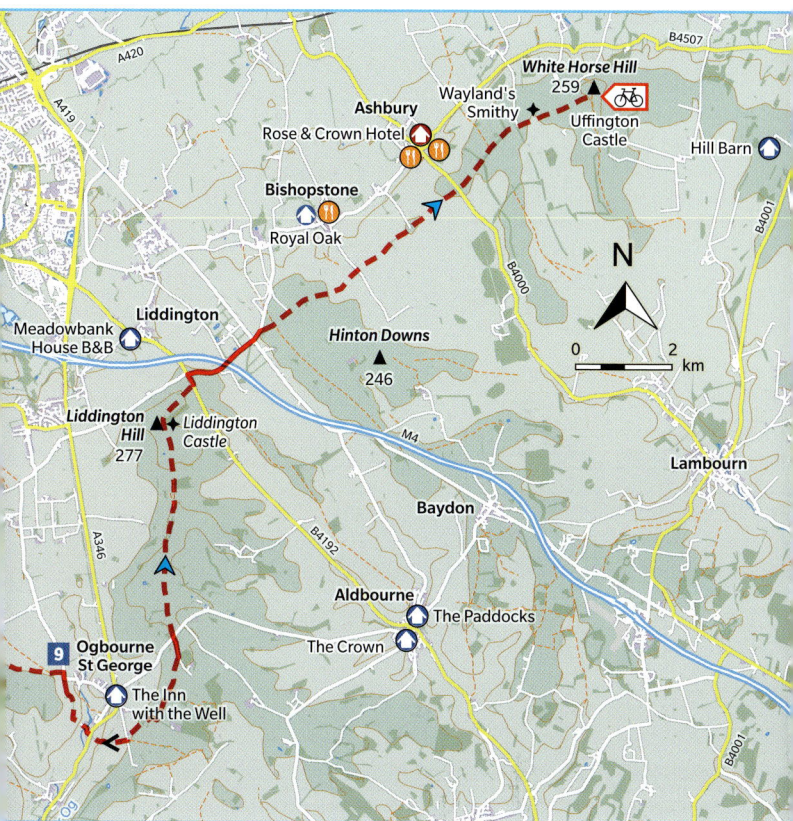

heading north–south; ignore them all and continue on the Ridgeway for 7km, past Wayland's Smithy, to **Uffington Castle**. Dating back to 600BCE, the earthworks at the National Trust site of Uffington Castle, on White Horse Hill, are well placed for a break.

> **Wayland's Smithy** is an early Neolithic chambered long barrow constructed around 3400BCE. Take a short detour from the route and inspect this atmospheric site, said to be the home of the Saxon 'God-Smith' known for his skill in making magical weaponry.

Sheep at dusk, Avebury Stone Circle

4 81% off road

Stage 4 – Ridgeway Part II and Thames Valley
Uffington Castle to Reading

Start/Finish	Uffington Castle/Reading Station (near)
Time	5–6hr
Total distance	48.8km (30.1 miles)
Off-road distance	39.2km
Percentage off-road	81%
Total ascent/descent	360/560m
Grade	Moderate ▲
Terrain	Singletrack 20%, track 61%, road 19%

As you head east towards the rising sun, the Vale of White Horse and the Thames Valley beyond dominate the skyline to the north. Below the Ridgeway, the historic birthplace of Alfred the Great, and the original seat of Wessex, Wantage, can be seen, and on a clear day you can make out Oxford on the horizon. The route continues on the Ridgeway to Streatley. Here the landscape changes as you meet the Thames and pick up the Thames Valley Path, heading south-east to Reading.

Summary table

Waypoint	Section	Distance	Ascent	Descent	Surface	Grade	Description
10	Uffington Castle – West Ilsley Ridgeway Car Park	19.4km	150m	220m	off-road	■	Easy rolling; great views in all directions
11	West Ilsley Ridgeway Car Park – Streatley	14.1km	120m	230m	off-road	■	Leaving the Ridgeway
12	Streatley – Reading Station (near)	15.3km	90m	110m	off-road	▲	Climbing on great singletrack before following the river valley into Reading

Uffington Castle to Reading

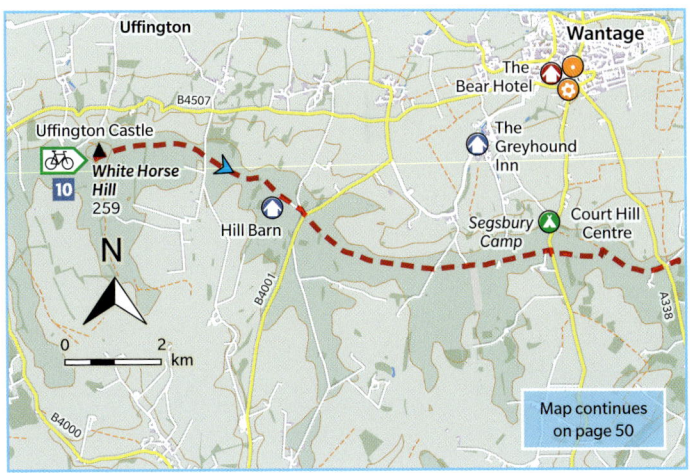

Directions

10 ■ Continue for a further 9km on the Ridgeway, ignoring all possible diversions, past Wantage to your north and the edge of Segsbury Camp. When you meet the A338, turn → and after 50m, turn ← back onto the Ridgeway. After 1km, past Whitehouse Farm, bear ← and after 50m turn → when you intersect with a restricted byway. After a short climb, fork ← and continue east on the Ridgeway for 7km to **West Ilsley Ridgeway car park**. If you are looking for refreshments, join the road where it intersects with West Ilsley Ridgeway car park and turn →, drop to West Ilsley and then continue to East Ilsley.

A quick snack stop at the Lord Wantage Monument

Stage 4 – Ridgeway Part II and Thames Valley

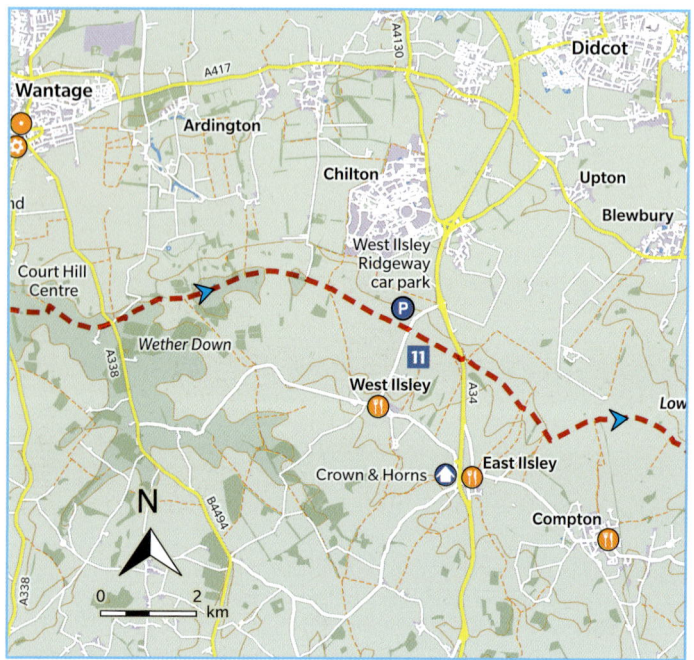

> Located just north of the route, **Segsbury Camp**, also known as Letcombe Castle, is a large Iron Age fort encompassing 30 acres. Excavations in 1871 revealed a stone-floored cist grave with flint walls. Perched on top of the Berkshire Downs, the fort offers sweeping views over the Vale of White Horse to the north.

11 ■ Continue for 1km and take a tunnel under the A34. After a further 1.5km, 1km east of East Ilsley, your route on the Ridgeway forks ←. After a further 2km it forks → and descends on Roden Downs before bearing ← and climbing up over Thurle Down. After exiting a small car park, you meet the road. Continue east for 2km, past the Goring & Streatley Golf Club, to the A329. Turn → and drop into **Streatley**, on the west bank of the Thames. Turn ← in the centre and head over the bridge into Goring. If you could do with a short day and a night off from camping, Streatley has a great youth hostel. The Pierreponts Café in Streatley is also a great pitstop option!

Uffington Castle to Reading

A late camp on the Ridgeway after dinner in East Ilsley

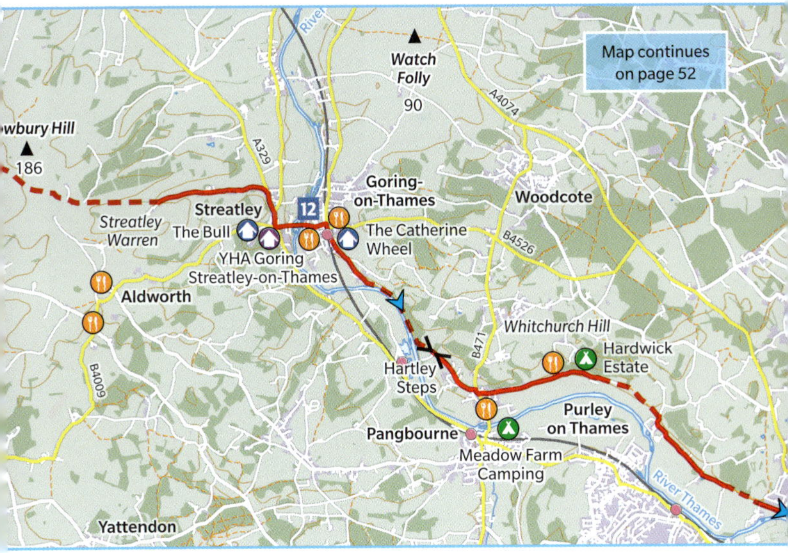

Stage 4 – Ridgeway Part II and Thames Valley

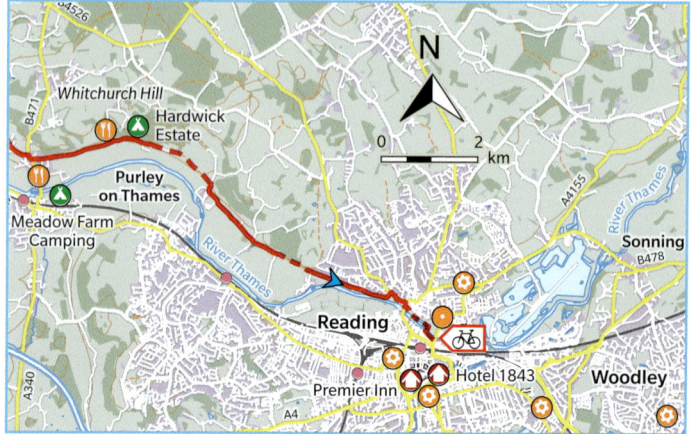

12 ▲ After you cross the railway, turn →, signed 'Crays Pond, Reading'. Ignore the next left onto the B4526 and after 750m fork → onto Gatehampton Road. Continue on this as it becomes the Thames Path and follow it for 1km when it bears ← and heads steeply into Lower Hartslock Wood. Hold your nerve as you drop steeply to the foot of the **Hartley Steps** then push up the other side. Continue to the B4471, turn → and, after 50m, bear ← onto Hardwick Road and continue on this for 2km.

When the road bears right, join a good asphalt bridleway ↑. This becomes a path after Hardwick House and you maintain your course to the road. Turn → and head through Mapledurham. Bear ← and continue on a good asphalt bridleway for 4km. Climb

Tough hauling yourself out from the Hartley Steps

Uffington Castle to Reading

past the church to the busy A4074, turn ➔ and descend. In Caversham, turn ➔ towards Caversham Bridge. Before reaching the bridge, turn ⬅ immediately after The Crown pub onto Promenade Road and pick up NCN 5. Continue towards the river and cross the Thames via a suspension bridge after Fry's Island. On the southern shore, immediately turn ⬅ onto NCN 5. The route hugs the Thames but this is the closest you get to Reading Station, the best place to extricate yourself back to London or west if you plan to break up the route or have to cut your trip short.

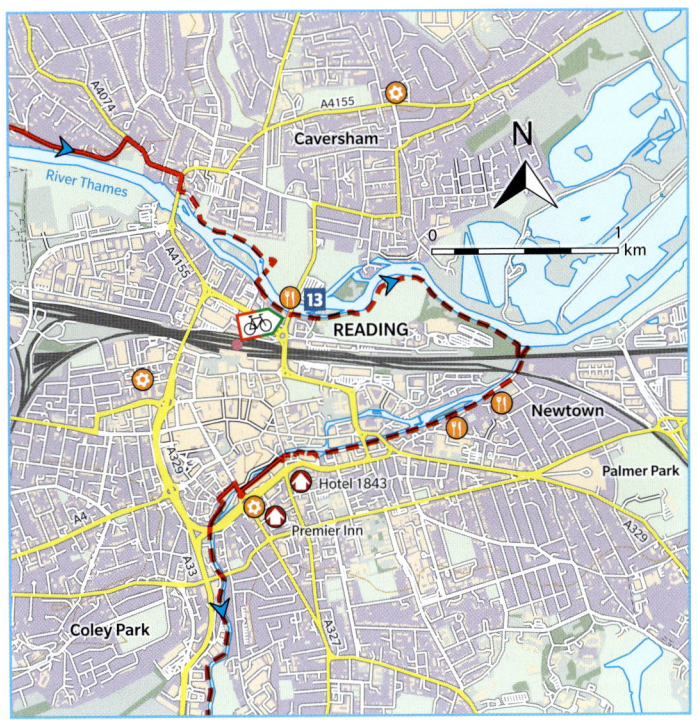

5 46% off road

Stage 5 – Forest of Eversley
Reading to Farnham

Start/Finish	Reading Station (near)/Farnham Castle
Time	4–6hr
Total distance	52.3km (32.5 miles)
Off-road distance	24.7km
Percentage off-road	46%
Total ascent/descent	360/350m
Grade	Easy ■
Terrain	Singletrack 9%, track 37%, road 54%
Note	This stage contains complex wayfinding to avoid Reading's busy urban centre. Broadly, you follow the Thames on NCN 5 and then join the River Kennet on NCN 4, heading west.

The highlights of this stage are less obvious; wayfinding becomes tiresome as you battle your way out of Reading, following the busy A33 and crossing the M4. Beyond here the countryside is a welcome departure from the noise and traffic, and you continue south into the historic area known as the Forest of Eversley, once the densely wooded site of a royal hunting forest but now largely given over to development. The route takes in Hazeley Heath and Odium Common, both remnants of the ancient woodland, before delivering you to Farnham Castle.

Summary table

Waypoint	Section	Distance	Ascent	Descent	Surface	Grade	Description
13	Reading Station (close to) – Three Mile Cross	11.7km	20m	20m	mixed	■	The most direct route out of Reading is still a challenge for way finding
14	Three Mile Cross – Riseley	7.6km	60m	40m	mixed	■	Bitty; unremarkable

Reading to Farnham

Waypoint	Section	Distance	Ascent	Descent	Surface	Grade	Description
15	Riseley – West Green	11.1km	70m	90m	mixed	■	The countryside is in sight
16	West Green – Dogmersfield	10.3km	70m	60m	mixed	■	Quiet roads and interesting common land
17	Dogmersfield – Farnham	11.6km	140m	140m	mixed	■	Prepare for a perfect descent into Farnham

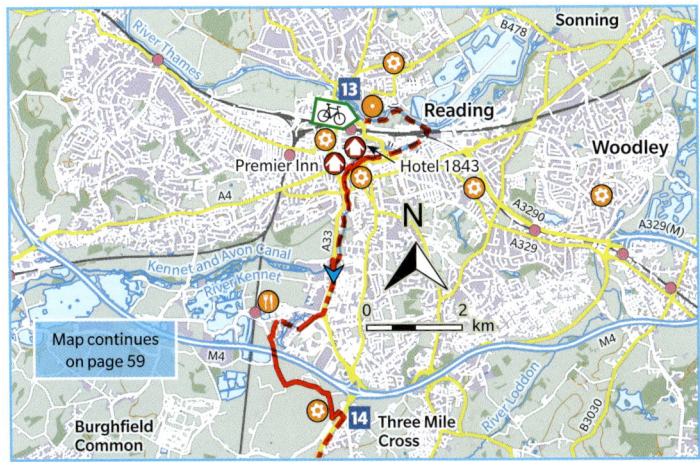

Directions

13 ■ Continue on NCN 5 as it follows the river for 1.5km to a footbridge. Here turn →, leave the Thames, head under **two railway bridges** and continue on the cycleway uninterrupted for 1.5km, as the path follows the left bank of the Kennet through the precincts that flank the river, to a big junction. Beyond the metal bollards, the route meets the busy Bridge Street. Turn ← and follow the blue cycleway NCN 23 signs for Newbury. Cross the road then turn → and head over the bridge. Now on the right bank on the river, turn ← onto Fobney Street. When you meet a patch of grass, turn ← to return to the river and then turn →. Maintain this course for 2km. After heading under a red brick bridge, the river swings →.

Following NCN5 along the Thames in Reading – a popular spot with pigeons

Stage 5 – Forest of Eversley

In the height of summer Reading precincts would be teaming with life

You now stop following the river and track the A33. After passing under the road, turn ➔, signed 'NCN 23', and leave the canal path on a sandy singletrack. On meeting the A33, walk south over the bridge and look for a sign on the ➔, 'R1, Town Centre 8 min'. Follow this back down, bear ➔ under the bridge and continue south alongside Foudry Brook for 1.5km as it bears ➔ under a large interchange. After a further 500m, NCN 23 turns ➔, signed 'Longwater Avenue', and continues over a metal bridge. At 100m after the bridge, leave NCN 23 and turn ← onto Longwater Avenue. After 100m, turn ➔ onto a gated asphalt drive with a blue cycleway sign and follow this to NCN 23 and Kirtons Farm Road. Turn ← and cross over the M4 motorway. You join Kybes Lane and then bear ← as your route becomes Hartley Court Road. After 1km bear ➔ onto Great Lea. On meeting the busy Mereoak Lane, turn ← and continue for 100m until the cycleway turns ➔, signposted 'Reading Town

Reading to Farnham

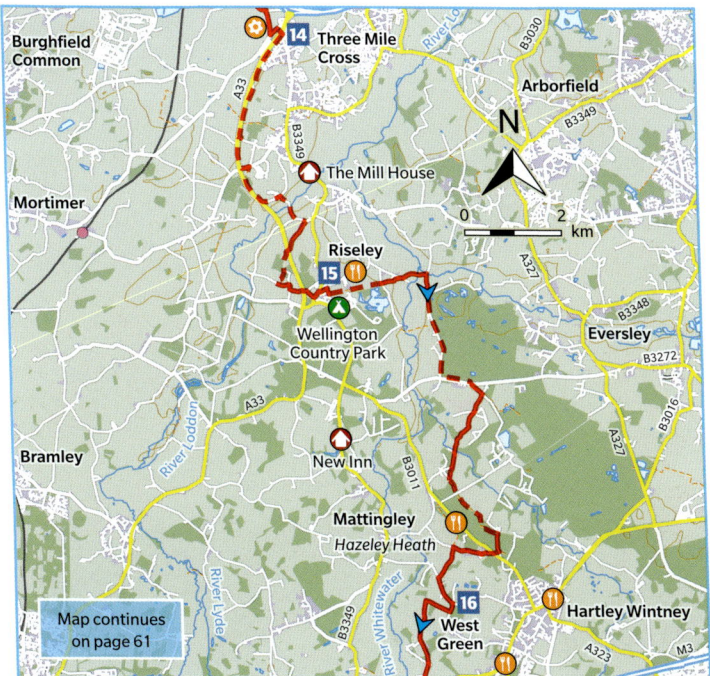

Centre' (don't worry, you aren't heading back into town). Continue for 50m to the junction.

14 ■ Cross the busy A33 via a pedestrian crossing. Now on the southbound dual carriageway, you are looking out for a gravel singletrack by a lamppost. Facing south with the track, take the ←; this delivers you onto an unrestricted byway running parallel to the road, heading south-west. Follow this poorly surfaced track for 2.5km.

Climb briefly on the bridleway up to Beech Hill Road as it spans the A33 and turn ←. After 100m, opposite Yew Tree lane, turn → onto a wide gravel bridleway. After 100m ignore the tunnel under the road and turn ← continuing on a bridleway that runs adjacent to the road for 1km before forking ← away from the bridleway on Lambs Lane.

Stage 5 – Forest of Eversley

Leave the road after 200m and turn → onto Kingsbridge Hill. At the first intersection, turn ← and at the second, turn → onto Spring Lane and follow this as it becomes a byway and spans the A33 once more. Continue until Bull Lane and turn ←. Follow this for 200m before forking ←, signed as a dead end. The path now goes through a tunnel under the A33. Shortly after the tunnel, turn → onto Sun Lane. When this meets the road just south of **Riseley**, turn ← and head towards the village before taking a → onto Norton Road. When you reach Odiham Road, turn →.

15 ■ Just to the left of the Riseley Village Tea Room, take a ← onto the Devil's Highway (old Roman road). Follow this for 1.5km before bearing → onto School Road. This becomes Part Lane and you continue to Bramshill, where you then turn → onto Ford Lane and continue south along the edge of Bramshill Plantation for 2km. Follow the track ← as it runs parallel with Bramshill Road for 450m. The main track continues east but the route turns → and takes an indistinct path through the wood, crossing Bramshill Road and joining Reading Drive South opposite the track. When this meets Plough Lane, turn → and continue for 1.5km towards Hazeley.

Blink and you'll miss it...an indistinct path takes you off Bramshill Plantation

Reading to Farnham

When the road bears right, take a small singletrack on the ← into a wood, indicated by a wooden signpost. After 100m at the intersection with a footpath you fork ← and continue past the impressive gatehouse of Bramshill House. Follow this path south for 1km, through **Hazeley Heath**, as it bears → and skirts two small ponds. After a further 300m, fork → onto a car-wide track. Continue south for 400m before taking a sharp → onto a narrow track that delivers you to the B3011. Cross the road and join Hazeley Bottom. After 1km, turn ← onto Stoken Lane, signed 'Dipley, West Green'. At the next junction turn ← and after 750m fork →, signed 'Phoenix Green'. After 100m turn →, signed 'Borough Court'.

16 ■ Follow the road as it bears sharply ← and continue for 2km until it meets London Road at Murrel Green. Turn ← and after 300m, opposite Mylbrook Used Cars, fork → onto Totters Lane. Follow this over the **railway** and then

Stage 5 – Forest of Eversley

under the M3. Bear → onto Potbridge Road. When you meet the B3016, continue ↑ for 900m before turning ← onto Bagwell Lane. After crossing Odiham Common for 1km, take an asphalt bridleway on the → through Swans Farm. Fork ← and take a footbridge over the Basingstoke Canal. Turn ← and join Sprat's Hatch Lane. Head north-east and cross the canal once more before turning sharply → by the Barley Mow pub onto Chatter Alley. Follow this on to **Dogmersfield**.

17 ■ With the Queens Head pub and phone box on your right, continue to Pilcot Road before bearing ← over a small red brick bridge. Continue into **Crookham Village**. In the centre, turn →, signed 'Crondall, Farnham'. Head past the Exchequer pub and over Chequers Bridge. Turn ←, taking a dead-end road onto Zephon Common Lane. When the road runs out, turn ←, cross the canal and continue for 100m, following the byway round to the →, and bear → as it re-crosses the canal once more. The track meets an asphalt road and you follow the bridleway past Albany Farm on the right. Continue along Watery Lane to Redfields Lane and turn ←. Continue ↑ at the roundabout for 200m before turning → onto Ewshot Lane.

After 300m turn ← onto a cycle track, crossing a small stream. Follow this as it bears right and continue ↑ for 1km until you reach Naishes Lane, where you turn →. Follow this back to Ewshot Lane and turn ←. After 400m, bear

Highland cattle calves! So cute

Reading to Farnham

Late Tudor extension of Farnham Castle

→ onto Church Lane, signed 'Farnham, Warren C'rner'. In 150m, with The Windmill pub on the left, fork ← past a phone box and continue uphill on a rough car-wide track to the B3013. Turn ← and then immediately turn → onto a rough track, blocked to vehicles by a gate, and turn → once more. Follow this track as it runs adjacent to the road and then bears ←, running alongside Odiham Road for 500m before you cross the road and join a bridleway on the →, Old Park Lane. Enjoy this exceptional descent, all the way to the moat of **Farnham Castle** and the A287.

> Built in the 12th century, **Farnham Castle** was formally home to Henri de Blois, Bishop of Winchester and grandson of William the Conqueror. The original building was demolished in the late 12th century by Henry II after the Anarchy and rebuilt over the following 200 years.

6

64% off road

Stage 6 – North Downs
Farnham to Forty Acre Lane

Start/Finish	Farnham Castle/Forty Acre Lane
Time	6–7hr
Total distance	59.4km (36.9 miles)
Off-road distance	37.9km
Percentage off-road	64%
Total ascent/descent	700/660m
Grade	Moderate ▲
Terrain	Singletrack 20%, track 44%, road 36%

Your journey south skirts the western edge of the North Downs, offering stunning heathland, wild singletrack and the iconic Devil's Punch Bowl – some of the most exciting riding on King Alfred's Way. The route follows the western edge of the Surrey Hills National Landscape, transitioning into a distinct lowland heathland habitat with heather, gorse and Scots pine. Most riding is on well-worn woodland tracks, but occasional deep sand requires caution. Wayfinding can be tricky without a GPX, as many trails are unmarked. Unlike the previous urban stages, settlements are sparse, so refill water bottles when possible. Campsites are limited, but wild camping is feasible at Frensham, Thursley, Hankley, Hindhead Commons and Torberry Hill, although these sensitive habitats require a light touch.

Summary table

Waypoint	Section	Distance	Ascent	Descent	Surface	Grade	Description
18	Farnham to Frensham Common	10.9km	120m	160m	mixed	■	Woodland singletrack heading to heathland common
19	Frensham Common to Thursley	11.4km	110m	70m	off-road	■	Very sandy in places!

Farnham to Forty Acre Lane

Waypoint	Section	Distance	Ascent	Descent	Surface	Grade	Description
20	Thursley to the Devil's Punch Bowl visitor centre	5.4km	170m	10m	off-road	🟩	Great views and welcome refreshment options
21	The Devil's Punch Bowl visitor centre to Bramshott	6.5km	10m	150m	paved	🟩	Descending parallel to the A3
22	Bramshott to Griggs Green	5.5km	30m	50m	mixed	🟩	Back into the woods
23	Griggs Green to Liss railway station	8.5km	50m	80m	mixed	🟩	Shipwrights Way over Weavers Down is a treat
24	Liss railway station to Forty Acre Lane	11.2km	210m	140m	mixed	🟩	Heading south towards the South Downs

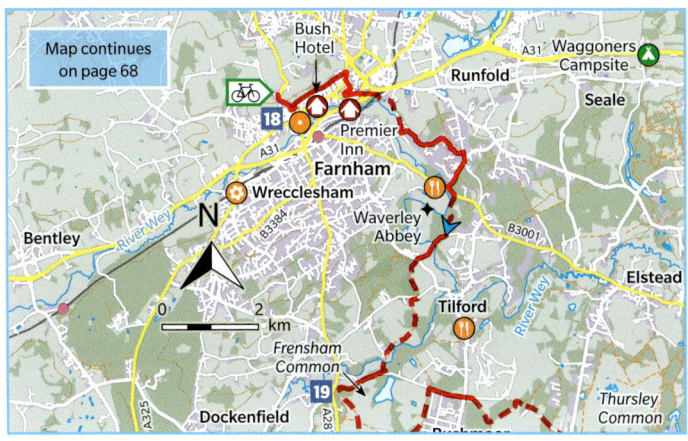

Directions

18 ■ Turn → and descend towards **Farnham** along Castle Street. With the Nelson Arms on your left, take a ← onto Park Row. After 80m turn onto a cobbled lane on your ←. In 25m, take the → fork and follow Scholars Way for 1km until it delivers you to the B3007 and the Six Bells Pub. Turn → and after 100m, at a busy junction, turn ← onto Manor Road. Follow this road, signed as a dead end, as it bears → past the hospital before delivering you to Guilford Road. Turn ← and continue towards the roundabout. On the → there is a foot tunnel;

Stage 6 – North Downs

Crossing the River Wey

take this into the centre of the roundabout, past the Shepherd and Flock pub, and follow NCN 22 along Moor Park Lane for 1km as it travels south. When you finally reach Compton Way, turn ← and continue on this as it bears → and takes you through Moor Park to Crooksbury Road. Turn → and after 100m, turn → onto Camp Hill and descend.

> Built in 1128, **Waverley Abbey** was the first Cistercian Abbey to be constructed in England by the then Bishop of Winchester, William Giffard. Like many others, the abbey was dissolved by King Henry VIII following his break from the Roman Catholic Church. The ruins of the abbey are worth a detour, and the café has a decent selection of refreshments.

Before Waverley Mill Bridge, at the T-junction, turn ← onto Waverley Lane (B3001), signed 'Godalming, Milford, Elstead'. After 200m, the road descends to the left, but you take the Greensand Way → into the wood. After 300m of rough track bearing ← through the wood, fork → and continue to the road. Turn →, descend on Sheephatch Lane and cross Tilford Mill Bridge. At the T-junction cross the road and join a bridleway that climbs up into the wood, bearing ←.

After 1km you are deposited on the road. Cross it and continue on the bridleway, signed 'Tilford Reeds', as it bears first → then ←. Continue on this across Tankersford Common for 1km, past Pierrepont Home Farm and over a footbridge. After a short climb, you enter the northern boundary of Frensham

Steep climbing on deep sand

Stage 6 – North Downs

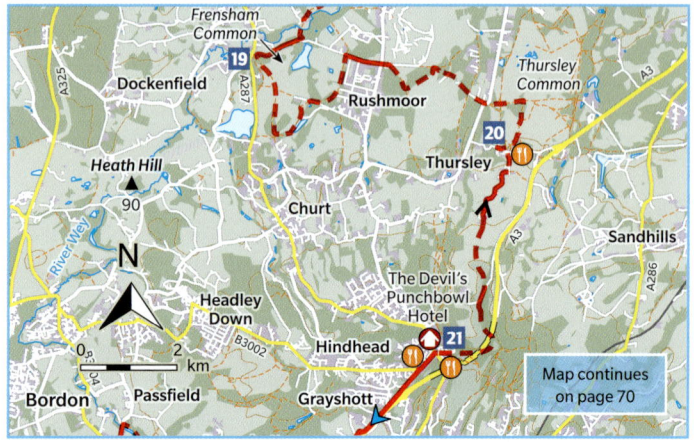

Common. Turn ➔ when you meet a byway and shortly join the road. In 500m the road bears sharply ➔ next to a car park on the edge of the wood. Here you continue ↑, following the edge of the wood, ignoring the more prominent byway heading south-east. After 300m tracking the edge of the wood, your route reaches an intersection with two bridleways heading south-east; take the first of these on your ← into **Frensham Common**. Frensham Common is a unique landscape and a good option for a wild camp if you tread lightly.

19 ■ Continue south across Frensham Common on a car-wide gravel track along the ridge that dissects the heathland. Large ponds are visible on both your left and right. After you have descended to the far edge of the wood, turn ← and continue for 1km to a footbridge and turn ➔ at the intersection with a second track to meet Sandy Lane. Follow this for 50m over a stream before forking ← opposite a small car park into the pine wood on a good car-wide bridleway. In 300m you meet a good cinder track on the westerly edge of **Rushmoor**. Follow this north for 1km to the road and turn ➔. After 1km cross Tilford Road and rejoin the bridleway. After 50m fork ➔ onto a bridleway and climb through the woods for 1km before taking a sharp ← and descending gradually before dropping into Lion's Mouth, a sandy patch of heathland where many paths converge. Yours is the most prominent path to your ➔, the Greensand Way, heading south-east.

Continue on this for 1.5km, past a car park, across Houndown Lane and past Hankley Common military training area, on your left. The road bears

Farnham to Forty Acre Lane

left and heads north and you follow a bridleway ↑, due east, onto Thursley Common. After 500m, take a → and climb steadily through Thursley National Nature Reserve. Fork → as you approach the top of the rise, → again as you start to descend and → a final time before dropping to the road. Turn ← and head into **Thursley**. The Three Horseshoes pub at Thursley is a good option for refreshments.

20 ■ With a phone box on your left, turn → towards the church. Follow the road to Little Cowdray Farm and continue uphill, ignoring routes to your left and right, rejoining the Greensand Way. Climb on this for 1km to Hindhead Commons as your route traverses the eastern shoulder of the Devil's Punch Bowl. Bearing →, and ignoring any options to the left, follow the ridge until it delivers you to the **Devil's Punch Bowl** visitor centre.

> **The Devil's Punch Bowl** is a thickly wooded natural amphitheatre, well-appointed with a visitor centre and café and a tap to fill up your bottles. Take time to read the chilling inscription on the Sailor's Stone as you skirt the edge of the Devil's Punch Bowl.

The Sailor's Stone marks the southern border of the Devil's Punch Bowl

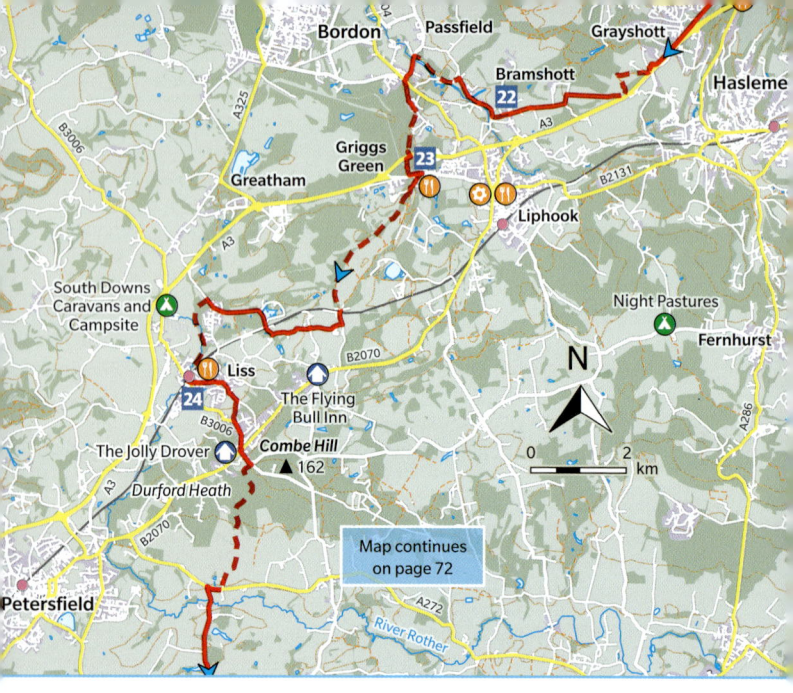

21 ■ Leave the visitor centre car park, pass the Devil's Punchbowl Hotel on your left and descend on London Road to the junction. Take the second exit, ↑, off the mini roundabout, signed 'London, Portsmouth', and descend on the A333. The BP garage on the A333 has an M&S. Continue ↑ at a second mini roundabout until you reach a major roundabout. Take the third exit, signed 'Bramshott Chase', and continue for 1km on Portsmouth Road. Give way at the gyratory and turn →. The fast road bears left, heading towards an underpass. Your route turns →, signed 'Shannon Court Road', and immediately turns ←, signed 'Bramshott Chase Lane'. Follow this as it climbs gently, bearing →, and then fork ← onto a bridleway. Continue for 500m before following the bridleway as it turns sharply ←. Descend steeply and follow the bridleway as it bears → across Bramshott Common. After 1km you meet the road and turn ← and then bear → onto Rectory Lane into **Bramshott**.

22 ■ When the road bears left, continue ↑ on to a byway opposite a large cream house. After 200m, you meet Tunbridge Lane and turn →. Continue ↑ for 800m to Bramshott Court before turning ← onto a bridleway. After 100m, take the → fork and continue ↑ for 1km when you rejoin the road. Turn ← on

Farnham to Forty Acre Lane

Passfield Road. At the junction turn →, signed 'Bordon', and then immediately ← onto a rough track. Take the bridleway that forks ← and continue on this into Conford. With the phone box on your right, turn → onto a bridleway, descend and cross a footbridge. Gently climb south for 500m, keeping ↑, then take a footbridge over the A3. Descend through a copse. The good track culminates at a locked gate, but the bridleway bears ← on a singletrack and is difficult to find. You meet the road at **Griggs Green**, on the outskirts of Liphook. The Deers Hut pub at Griggs Green is a possible food option.

23 ■ Turn ← and then immediately turn →, with the Deers Hut pub on your left. Follow signs for the Shipwrights Way and take the byway on the → into the wood. You now follow the Shipwrights Way south for 3km to Langley and cross the **railway** on a road bridge. After 200m turn → onto NCN 22, signed 'Shipwrights Way, Liss'. Continue for 1.5km, bear → and take a tunnel under the railway. Bear ← as you skirt around the west bank of a lake on Warren Road for 1km. After a further 1km on Forest Road, follow NCN 22 ← as it turns into the wood once more. Continue for 2km, over a footbridge and past

A magical atmosphere in the early evening on Durford Heath

Stage 6 – North Downs

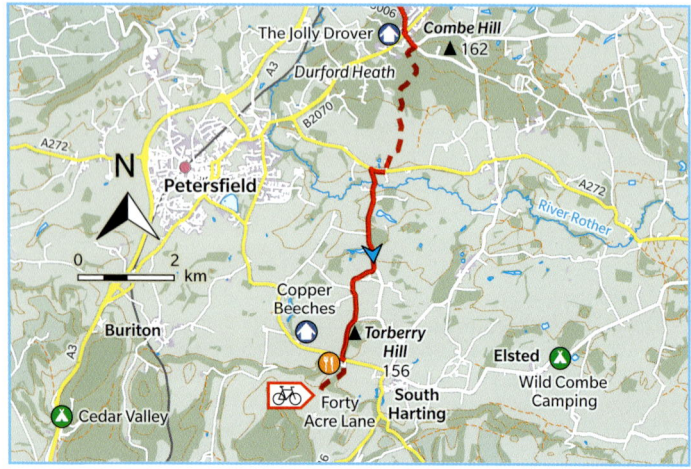

Liss railway station. Turtle Bean Café on Station Road in Liss is a favourite with cyclists. Durleighmarsh Farm Shop is also a possible food option.

24 ■ Turn ← over the level crossing. Continue along the main street to the mini roundabout. Take the second ←, past the Whistle Stop pub, onto Station Road and, after 200m, fork → onto Rake Road. Continue on this for 800m before forking → onto Huntsbottom Lane. Bear ← and continue for 300m before forking → onto Woodlands Lane. Descend to Hill Brow Road, turn ← and continue for 500m to the junction. Turn → and then immediately ←, signed 'Rogate', at the Jolly Drover pub. After 200m, at the Durford Wood car park, turn → onto a gated bridleway. Follow the Sussex Border Path bridleway over Durford Heath for 2.5km, past Durleighmarsh Farm Shop, until it meets the A272.

Cross the road and turn → to join a lane running parallel with it. After 200m, turn ← and follow Collins Lane over a bridge crossing the River Rother and continue for 2km. Fork → for Quebec. Continue along Torberry Lane, on the Sussex Border Path route, to the B2146. Turn ← and then immediately → by a little post box; you have reached Torberry Hill. Follow the road around the shoulder of **Torberry Hill**. At the junction with the B2146, turn ← and immediately → and bear → along the base of Hemner Hill and climb. Continue for 700m to the intersection of two tracks and turn → onto the rougher restricted byway, **Forty Acre Lane**. You are now on the South Downs Way.

74% off road

7

Stage 7 – South Downs

Forty Acre Lane to Winchester

Start/Finish	Forty Acre Lane/King Alfred Statue, Winchester
Time	4hr 30min–6hr
Total distance	51.2km (31.8 miles)
Off-road distance	37km
Percentage off-road	74%
Total ascent/descent	740/790m
Grade	Moderate ▲
Terrain	Singletrack 41%, track 33%, road 26%

You're now on the home straight, looking west once more with your focus on the prize: the historic capital of the long-extinct kingdom of Wessex. This final stage, arguably the toughest, never fails to deliver. Once you gain the South Downs Way, your first challenge is Queen Elizabeth Country Park and the imposing Butser Hill beyond. From there this isolated rolling landscape continues to test the rider, heading past Old Winchester Hill, the site of an Iron Age hill fort once occupied by the Celtic Belgae tribe, and on to Twyford Down, St Catherine's Hill and the southern gate of the city.

Summary table

Waypoint	Section	Distance	Ascent	Descent	Surface	Grade	Description
25	Forty Acre Lane – Queen Elizabeth Country Park visitor centre	11.2km	140m	160m	off-road	▲	Climbing on wide gravel tracks
26	Queen Elizabeth Country Park visitor centre – Old Winchester Hill	13.1km	260m	190m	mixed	▲	Butser Hill!
27	Old Winchester Hill – Beacon Hill Nature Reserve	7.2km	140m	190m	mixed	■	Stunning rolling landscape and good trails

Stage 7 – South Downs

Waypoint	Section	Distance	Ascent	Descent	Surface	Grade	Description
28	Beacon Hill Nature Reserve – Cheesefoot Head	9.5km	130m	160m	off-road	🟩	The South Downs Way is a gravel-rider's dream
29	Cheesefoot Head – King Alfred Statue, Winchester	10.2km	70m	90m	mixed	🟩	Nice descents and your goal is in sight

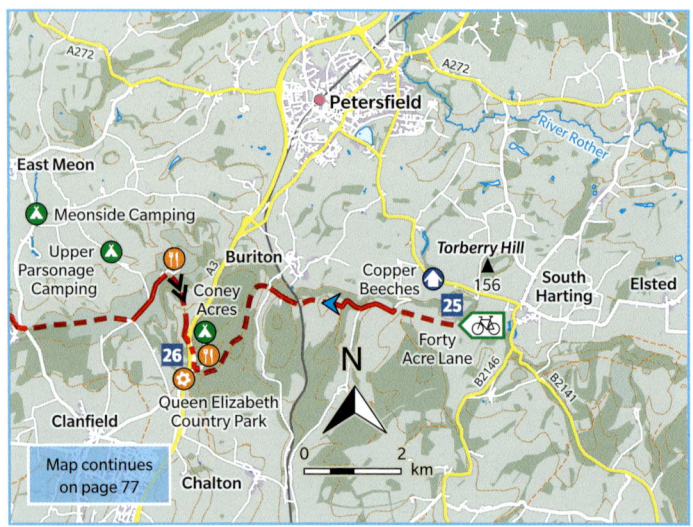

Directions

25 ▲ After 1km the track meets a road at Sunwood Farm. Turn ← and follow the road through the farmyard, continuing west as the road bears →, following the road and forking →. After 100m bear ← and descend steeply and then bear → past Coulters Dean and climb on the good gravel track until it rejoins a road after Dean Barn. At the junction with Kiln Lane, you reach Halls Hill car park. Cross the car park and head through a metal gate onto a gravel track. Bear sharply ← and begin to climb steeply into the woods of **Queen Elizabeth Forest** continuing on the SDW (South Downs Way). Take care to follow signs for the SDW rather than the Shipwrights Way once you enter the Queen Elizabeth Forest. The woods also contain a variety of graded

Forty Acre Lane to Winchester

Checking the map at the foot of Old Winchester Hill

MTB runs – and it's easy to find yourself on one! You descend steeply through the woods and your route meets asphalt once more near the park's southern entrance. When your track meets the road, turn ← and descend gently to the car park, then turn → and continue north on the SDW on asphalt, past the Queen Elizabeth Park visitor centre on your right. Queen Elizabeth Country Park visitor centre is a great place to refuel.

26 ▲ After you pass the car barrier, a shallow climb leads to a junction and you turn →, signed 'Petersfield', and continue under a bridge that spans the **A3**. Bear → and then turn ← onto an asphalt track that continues on the SDW. Climb steeply up the southern nose of Butser Hill, which is a challenge for even the widest MTB gearing! You top out and bear ←, shortly passing the Roundhouse Café, an ideal stop for well-deserved refreshments. Beyond here bear ← onto Limekiln Lane and descend south for 900m. At the intersection with a second road, take the first → onto North Lane and continue west on the SDW, past South Downs Equine Therapy Centre, for 2km. When you rejoin the road, continue ↑, signed 'Droxford, Warnford', on the Droxford Road. After 50m follow the road, signed 'Sustainability Centre, Droxford'.

The stars from my camp in the woods

Forty Acre Lane to Winchester

The Sustainability Centre, an independent learning and study centre, offers camping at **South Downs Eco Lodge and Campsite**, a good option for an overnight. If you are wild camping, head into Hen Wood west of East Meon; the mixed woodland is flat and spacious at the summit.

Hug the shoulder of Wether Down for 700m before making a sharp → turn onto a track marked as unsuitable for vehicles. Follow the SDW on a byway for 2km to the road at Coombe Cross. Rejoin the byway and continue north on Halnaker Lane for 600m before following the SDW as it forks sharply ← and descends to Meon Springs Trout Fishery. Turn → and after 300m, turn ← with the SDW and continue over a bridge through Whitewool Farm. Continue on a good car-wide track, through a gate, and turn → before climbing steeply on a rough track to the road. Turn sharply ← and continue along the high ridge of **Old Winchester Hill** on a path that flanks the road, with breathtaking views on either side. This large area of access land could make an excellent location for a wild camp but avoid the open summit or you may well be woken very early by the nature reserve warden!

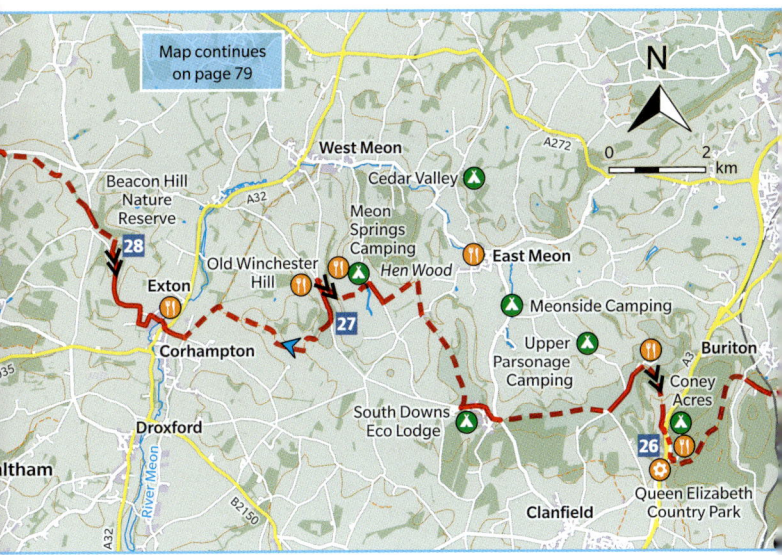

Stage 7 – South Downs

27 ■ As the path diverges from the road, bear → and maintain the high ground before descending steeply, with the location of the old fort to your right. Halfway down the hill the SDW forks →. After 500m turn → and then, after 100m, turn ←. Descend to a disused railway line, turn ← and follow it south for 600m. Leave the railway track and descend to the road. Turn → through the remains of the red brick railway bridge before turning ← at the junction. On reaching the A32, continue at this staggered junction onto Beacon Hill Lane into **Exton**. With the Shoe Inn on your right, take the ← onto Beacon Hill Lane. Follow as the flint-wall-flanked Allens Farm Lane bears first ← and then sharply →. After 100m, turn → and follow the SDW as it joins the White Way and forks → to climb Beacon Hill. After topping out, you turn ←, descend to a junction and follow the road as it bears → and then ← at the **Beacon Hill Nature Reserve** car park.

28 ■ After a further 150m, the road bears right but you continue ↑, through a gate, along the SDW. Follow this through Lomer Farm and then bear → and continue past Wind Farm before joining Wheely Down Farm Lane and continuing to the junction. Turn →, signed 'Winchester'. After 100m, fork ← onto Holden Lane and follow the SDW. Descend and follow this good track for 2km through Holden Farm and across the A272. There's a great cyclists' café and campsite at Holden Farm. Climb the track and turn →. After 100m, turn ← and maintain your course on the SDW. Climb over Gander Down on the Allan

The Handlebar Café outside Winchester

Forty Acre Lane to Winchester

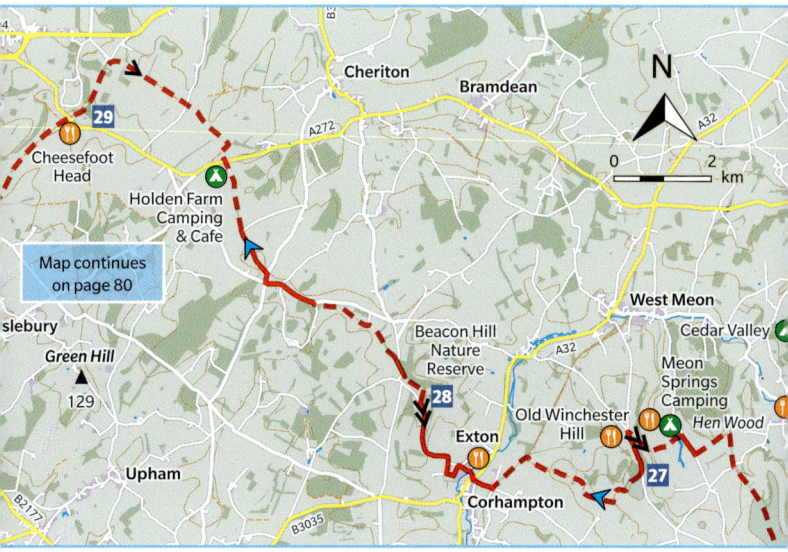

King Way and continue ↑, travelling north-west for 2km to Keeper's Cottage. Turn ← and climb before descending. Climb to the road and **Cheesefoot Head** on the SDW.

> **Cheesefoot Head** is a natural amphitheatre, famously the muster point for the Allied troops. It was here that General Dwight Eisenhower made his famous speech to American troops on 6 June 1944 before the D-Day landings.

29 ■ Continue to the road, turn → and then immediately ← onto a rough track heading over an open field. Descend down the nose of Fawley Down until you meet a good track that becomes Fawley Lane and then continue to the road. Cross Morestead Road and join Hazeley Road. After 1km, turn → and climb to the war memorial. Bear ← here and follow the Pilgrims' Trail north-west, across open land, over Twyford Down. Descend and take a bridge over the M3. Fork ← and enjoy a swooping descent around the southern shoulder of St Catherine's Hill. Turn → when you meet the Itchen Way and follow the course of the river north to the Garnier Road car park. Turn → and continue under the arch by the **Handlebar Café**, then turn ← at the entrance to St Catherine's Hill

Stage 7 – South Downs

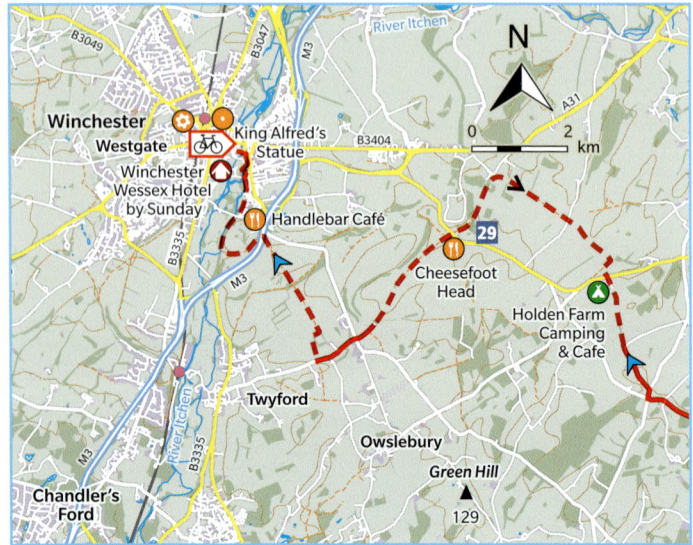

Park and follow the old railway track towards town. When this meets Domum Road, continue to the junction and turn ➔ along Wharf Hill. After 100m, turn ⬅ and shortly ➔ over a small bridge. Follow the river past Wolvesey Palace to the road and turn ⬅ at the Bishop on the Bridge Pub. Your goal is in sight: the **statue of King Alfred the Great**. Take some photos and enjoy a rest – you've earned it!

At the foot of King Alfred's statue

Appendix A
Accommodation

Stage	Waypoint	Location	Name	Type	Tel
1	1	Winchester	Winchester Wessex Hotel by Sunday	🏠	+44 1962 861611
	3	Middle Winterslow	Little Buckholt Farm	🏠	+44 7967 916988
	3	Pitton	White Hill Farm Caravanning Park	⛺	+44 1722 712367
	3	Salisbury	Salisbury North Bishopdown Premier Inn	⛺	+44 1722 320713
	3	Salisbury	Salisbury Camping and Caravan Club site	🏠	+44 333 3218461
2	4	High Post	The Stones Hotel	🏠	+44 1722 782020
	4	Lake	Finch Cottage B&B	🏠	+44 7837 025545
	5	Amesbury	Robin Hill Cottage	🏠	+44 7831 873262
	5	Amesbury	The George Hotel – Amesbury	🏠	+44 1980 622108
	5	Amesbury	Fairlawn House	🏠	+44 1980 622103
	5	Amesbury	Travelodge Amesbury	🏠	+44 871 9846218
	5	Winterbourne Stoke	Stonehenge Campsite & Glamping Pods	⛺	+44 7786 734732
	5	Orcheston	Stonehenge Touring Park	⛺	+44 7999 867040
	5	Cholderton	Stonehenge Hostel	🏠	+44 1980 629438
	6	Tilshead	Brades Acre Campsite	⛺	+44 1980 620402
	6	Tilshead	West View B&B	🏠	+44 7729 702181
	6	Market Lavington	The Green Dragon	🏠	+44 1380 813235
3	7	All Cannings	Little Owls Camping	⛺	+44 1380 848253
	7	Honey Street	Well Cottage	🏠	+44 7880 785895
	7	East Kennet	Ridgeway Campsite	⛺	+44 7775 524197
	7	Marlborough	Postern Hill Campsite	⛺	+44 1672 515195
	8	Avebury	Avebury Life	🏠	+44 1672 539644
	8	Winterbourne Monkton	New Inn	🏠	+44 1672 539793

Appendix A – Accommodation

🟣 hostel   🟢 campsite   🔵 B&B   🔴 hotel   🟩 self-catering/glamping

Web/email	Comments
mercure-wessex.choice-hotels-winchester.co.uk	Good bike storage
whitehillfarmcaravanpark.co.uk	3km south of route, just off the Monarch's Way
premierinn.com	1km south of the route
campingandcaravanningclub.co.uk/campsites/uk/wiltshire/salisbury/salisbury-camping-and-caravanning-club-site	1km south of Old Sarum
thestoneshotel.co.uk	2km east of the route
finchcottage.co.uk	
george-amesbury.co.uk	
alittleplace.co.uk	
travelodge.co.uk	
stonehengecampsite.co.uk	8km west of Amesbury
stonehengetouringpark.com	
stonehengehostel.co.uk	5km east of Amesbury
bradesacre.co.uk	Close to the route; off the A360
welcomewestview.co.uk	
wadworth.co.uk	1km west of the route
littleowlscamping.co.uk	1km south of All Cannings
wellcottagehoneystreet.co.uk	4km east of All Cannings
ridgewaycampsite.com	
posternhillcamping.co.uk	10km east of the route, south of Marlborough
avebourylife.com	
elderbrookhouse.com	North of Avebury, off A361

Bikepacking King Alfred's Way

Stage	Waypoint	Location	Name	Type	Tel
	9	Ogbourne St George	The Inn with the Well	⬤	+44 1672 841445
	9	Aldbourne	The Crown	⬤	+44 1672 540214
	9	Aldbourne	The Paddocks	⬤	+44 7712 304529
	9	Liddington	Meadowbank B&B	⬤	+44 1793 791401
	9	Bishopstone	Royal Oak	⬤	+44 1793 790481
	9	Ashbury	Rose & Crown Hotel	⬤	+44 1793 378354
	9	Uffington	Oxford Oak Camping	⬤	+44 7482 044040
4	10	Kingston Lisle	Nordic Glamping Ltd	⬤	+44 7712 880021
	10	Sparsholt Firs	Hill Barn	⬤	+44 7885 368918
	10	Letcombe Regis	The Greyhound Inn	⬤	+44 1235 771969
	10	Wantage	The Bear Hotel	⬤	+44 1235 766366
	10	Letcombe Basset	Court Hill Centre	⬤	+44 1235 760253
	11	East Ilsley	Crown & Horns	⬤	+44 1635 281545
	11	Didcot	St Peter's Campsite	⬤	+44 7794 175307
	12	Highcroft	Ridgeway View Campsite	⬤	+44 7552 533381
	12	Streatley	YHA Streatley and Goring	⬤	+44 345 3719044
	12	Streatley	The Bull	⬤	+44 1491 872392
	12	Goring	The Catherine Wheel	⬤	+44 1491 872379
	12	Pangbourne	Meadow Farm Camping	⬤	+44 7912 068720
	12	Hardwick	Hardwick Estate	⬤	+44 118 9842955
5	13	Reading	Premier Inn Reading	⬤	+44 871 5278924
	13	Reading	Hotel 1843	⬤	+44 118 9503925
	14	Swallowfield	The Mill House Hotel	⬤	+44 118 9883124
	15	Riseley	Wellington Country Park	⬤	+44 118 9326444
	15	Heckfield	The New Inn Heckfield	⬤	+44 118 9326374
	16	Greywell	Fox & Goose Pub & Campsite	⬤	+44 1256 702062
	17	Farnham	Waggoners Campsite	⬤	+44 7385 812842
	17	Farnham	Premier Inn Farnham	⬤	+44 333 2346490
	17	Farnham	Bush Hotel	⬤	+44 1252 715237

Appendix A – Accommodation

Web/email	Comments
thewellguesthouse.co.uk	No longer a pub, just a guesthouse, but great food options
	4km east of the route
1thepaddocks.co.uk	*4km east of the route*
meadowbankhouse.com	Near the route, south of Swindon
helenbrowningsorganic.co.uk	*1km north of the route*
roseandcrownatashbury.co.uk	Village pub and inn
theoxfordoakcamping.co.uk	*5km north of the route*
nordicglampingatbotswicky.co.uk	*2km north of the route*
hillbarnbedandbreakfast.co.uk	*1km south of the route*
thegreyhoundletcombe.co.uk	*2.5km north of the route*
thebearwantage.co.uk	*4km north of the route*
courthill.org.uk	Just north of the route
crownandhorns.co.uk	*4km south of the route*
ukcampsite.co.uk/sites/details.asp?revid=8728	East of Didcot
ridgewayadventures.co.uk/camping	*7km north of the route*
yha.org.uk/hostel/yha-streatley-on-thames	
bullinnpub.co.uk	
tcwgoring.co.uk	
meadowfarmcamping.com	Cross the Thames for Pangbourne
hardwickestate.co.uk/riverside-campsite/	Located on the northern bank of the Thames
premierinn.com/gb/en/hotels/england/berkshire/reading/reading-central.html	
1843reading.com	
themillhousehotel.co.uk	*2km east of the route*
wellingtoncountrypark.co.uk	
newinnheckfield.com	*3km east of the route*
	4km east of Whitehall
waggonerscampsite.co.uk	*5km east of the end of Stage 14*
premierinn.com/gb/en/hotels/england/surrey/farnham/farnham.html	
farnhambush.com	

Bikepacking King Alfred's Way

Stage	Waypoint	Location	Name	Type	Tel
6	21	Hindhead	The Devil's Punchbowl Hotel	🏠	+44 1428 606565
	24	Liss	The Flying Bull Inn	🏠	+44 1730 892285
	24	Liss	South Downs Caravans and campsite	⛺	+44 1730 894182
	24	Hill Brow	The Jolly Drover	🏠	+44 1730 893137
	24	Western Weald	Night Pastures	⛺	+44 1428 610120
	24	Petersfield	Copper Beeches	🏠	+44 1730 826662
	24	Elsted	Wild Combe Camping	⛺	+44 7775 568415
7	25	Butser Hill	Coney Acres	⛺	+44 23 92595040
	26	East Meon	Upper Parsonage Farm	⛺	+44 7769 860889
	26	East Meon	Meonside Camping	⛺	
	26	East Meon	Cedar Valley	⛺	+44 7557 798857
	26	East Meon	South Downs Eco Lodge	⛺	+44 1730 823549
	26	Meon Springs	Meon Springs	🏠⛺	+44 1730 823134
	28	Cheriton	Holden Farm Camping and Café	⛺	+44 7599 553740

Appendix A – Accommodation

Web/email	Comments
devilspunchbowlhotel.co.uk	
theflyingbull.com	*2km south of the route from Langley*
	1km north of Liss Station
thejollydrover.co.uk	
nightpastures.com	*5km east of the route towards Fernhurst*
copperbeeches.net	
wildcombecamping.co.uk	*3km east of the route*
qecp.enquiries@hants.gov.uk	located at Queen Elizabeth Country Park
upperparsonagefarm.co.uk	800m from the route, after Butser Hill
meonsidecamping.weebly.com	East Meon has a great pub!
cedarvalley.co.uk	*2km north of the route*
sustainability-centre.org/south-downs-eco-lodge.html	
meonsprings.com	
holdenfarm.co.uk	Also has refreshments

Appendix B
Bike shops

Winchester

BikeX
Silver Hill, Winchester SO23 8AE
+44 1962 868914
uk.bikex.store

Chase Cycles
3–4 Upper High St, Winchester SO23 8UT
+44 1962 807300
chase-cycles.co.uk

Salisbury

Hayball Cyclesport
26–30 Winchester St, Salisbury SP1 1HG
+44 1722 411378
hayballcyclesport.co.uk

Stonehenge Cycles
86 Fisherton St, Salisbury SP2 7QY
+44 1722 334915
stonehengecycles.com

Halfords Salisbury
Unit L, Dairy Meadow Ln, Salisbury SP1 2TJ
halfords.com

Amesbury

Hills Cycles and Fishing Tackle
Smithfield St, Amesbury, Salisbury SP4 7AL
+44 1980 622705
hillscycles.wixsite.com/hillscycles

Shrewton

Funky Velo
Hill House, Nett Rd, Shrewton, Salisbury SP3 4HB
+44 7795 567927
funkyvelobikes@gmail.com

Devizes

Bikes 'n' Boards
121 Southbroom Rd, Devizes SN10 1LY
+44 1380 729621
bikesnboards@hotmail.co.uk

Marlborough

The Marlborough Bike Company
1–2 Kingsbury St, Marlborough SN8 1HU
+44 1672 515156
marlboroughbike.co.uk

Swindon

Mitchell Cycles
27 Shrivenham Rd, Swindon SN1 2QA
+44 1793 523306
mitchellcycles.co.uk

Appendix B – Bike shops

Swindon Cycles
60A Beechcroft Rd, Swindon SN2 7QD
+44 1793 700105
swindoncycles.co.uk

Cyclecare
89 High St., Purton, Swindon SN5 4AB
+44 1793 778123
cyclecareswindon.co.uk

Wantage

Ridgeway Cycles
22 Newbury St, Wantage OX12 8DA
+44 1235 764445
ridgewaycycles.com

Reading

Berkshire Cycle Co.
186 Loddon Bridge Rd, Woodley,
Reading RG5 4BS
+44 118 969 5776
berkshirecycles.co.uk

Reading Bike Kitchen
Unit C10, Weldale St, Reading RG1 7BX
readingbicyclekitchen.org

MT-cycle repairs
41 Norris Rd, Reading RG6 1NJ
+44 7519 684766
mkdt1989.wixsite.com/mt-cyclerepairs

Evans Cycles
Mill Ln, Reading RG1 2HN
+44 343 909 2117
evanscycles.com/
reading-ev-store-2117

AW Cycles
110 Henley Rd, Reading RG4 6DH
+44 118 946 3050
awcycles.co.uk

Pete's Bike Shed
1 Farm Cottages, Three Mile Cross,
Reading RG7 1NX
+44 7760 197307
petesbikeshed.co.uk

Farnham

Hoops Velo
Unit E, Grovebell Retail Park,
Wrecclesham Rd, Wrecclesham,
Farnham GU10 4PL
+44 1252 448836
hoopsvelo.com

Liphook

Liphook Cycles
16 The Square, Liphook GU30 7AH
+44 1428 727858
liphookcycles.com

Queen Elizabeth Country Park

Southern eBike Rentals
Queen Elizabeth Country Park,
Waterlooville PO8 0QE
+44 23 9241 4624
southernebikerentals.co.uk

Bikepacking King Alfred's Way

Appendix C
Recommended kit lists

Essential kit list

This is a suggestion of what you'll need if you're relying on local facilities for food and staying at a campsite.

Clothes
- Padded shorts x 2
- Off-road cycling shoes, trainers or trail shoes
- 2 pairs of socks
- Long-sleeved top
- Short-sleeved top
- Waterproof jacket
- Helmet

Repair kit
- 2 x Inner tubes for your tyres
- Tyre levers
- Multitool
- Chain tool and spare link
- Puncture repair kit
- Pump

Camping equipment
- Tent or bivvy bag
- Sleeping bag
- Sleeping mat
- Inflatable pillow
- Head torch

Other
- Water bottle(s)
- First aid kit (antiseptic wipes, plasters)
- Mobile phone (provide alternative means of navigation as well)
- Lights (to see by and be seen by)
- A spare battery for lights
- Power pack to charge lights, phone, etc.
- Electrolytes
- Toilet roll
- Shovel
- Map
- Compass
- Micro rucksack

Extended list

As well as the items on the essential list, the following list is a suggestion of what you'll need if you are going out of season or plan to be fully self-supported (not using local facilities and campsites).

Clothes
- Waterproof gloves
- SealSkinz® waterproof socks
- Warm hat
- Arm warmers
- Thermal leggings
- Down/synthetic down jacket
- Full-length padded leggings
- Snood

Appendix C – Recommended kit lists

Repair kit
- Spare chain
- Spare tyre
- CO_2 Gas canisters and dispenser
- Oil
- Rag

Other
- Cycling computer
- Backup power pack
- Tarp and hammock set-up
- Gas stove
- Pot
- Mug
- Coffee equipment/Coffee
- Food for the duration
- Water filter
- Camping knife/Leatherman
- Flint lighter (matches can get wet)
- Long spork
- Dry bags
- Cash

Download the GPX files

All the routes in this guide are available for download from:

cicerone.co.uk/1238/GPX

as standard format GPX files. You should be able to load them into most online GPX systems and mobile devices, whether GPS or smartphone. You may need to convert the file into your preferred format using a conversion programme such as gpsvisualizer.com or one of the many other such websites and programmes.

When you follow this link, you will be asked for your email address and where you purchased the guidebook, and have the option to subscribe to the Cicerone e-newsletter.

cicerone.co.uk

LISTING OF CICERONE GUIDES

BRITISH ISLES CHALLENGES, COLLECTIONS AND ACTIVITIES
Great Walks on the England Coast Path
Map and Compass
The Big Rounds
The Book of the Bivvy
The Book of the Bothy
The Mountains of England and Wales
  Vol 1 — Wales
  Vol 2 — England
The National Trails
Walking the End to End Trail
Cycling Land's End to John o' Groats

LAKE DISTRICT
Bikepacking in the Lake District
Cycling in the Lake District
Joss Naylor's Lakes, Meres and Waters of the Lake District
Lake District Winter Climbs
Lake District: High Level and Fell Walks
Lake District: Low Level and Lake Walks
Mountain Biking in the Lake District
Outdoor Adventures with Children — Lake District
Scrambles in the Lake District — North
Scrambles in the Lake District — South
Trail and Fell Running in the Lake District
Walking The Cumbria Way
Walking the Lake District Fells
  — Borrowdale
  — Buttermere
  — Coniston
  — Keswick
  — Langdale
  — Mardale and the Far East
  — Patterdale
  — Wasdale
Walking the Tour of the Lake District

NORTH-WEST ENGLAND AND THE ISLE OF MAN
Walking the King Charles III England Coast Path: North West
Walking the King Charles III England Coast Path: North West
  — Cumbria Map Booklet
  — Lancashire and Merseyside Map Booklet
Cycling the Pennine Bridleway
Walking the Pennine Way
Walking the Pennine Way Map Booklet
Isle of Man Coastal Path
The Lune Valley and Howgills
Walking in Cumbria's Eden Valley
Walking in Lancashire
Walking in the Forest of Bowland and Pendle
Walking on the Isle of Man
Walking on the West Pennine Moors
Walking the Ribble Way
Hadrian's Wall Path
Hadrian's Wall Path Map Booklet
The Coast to Coast Cycle Route
The Coast to Coast Map Booklet
The Coast to Coast Walk

NORTH-EAST ENGLAND, YORKSHIRE DALES AND PENNINES
Walking the Dales Way
The Dales Way Map Booklet
Cycling the Reivers Route
Cycling the Way of the Roses
Cycling in the Yorkshire Dales
Great Mountain Days in the Pennines
Mountain Biking in the Yorkshire Dales
The Cleveland Way and the Yorkshire Wolds Way
The Cleveland Way Map Booklet
The North York Moors
Trail and Fell Running in the Yorkshire Dales
Walking in County Durham
Walking in Northumberland
Walking in Northumberland
Walking in the North Pennines
Walking in the Yorkshire Dales
  — North and East
  — South and West
Walking St Cuthbert's Way
Walking St Oswald's Way and Northumberland Coast Path

DERBYSHIRE, PEAK DISTRICT AND MIDLANDS
Cycling in the Peak District
Dark Peak Walks
Scrambles in the Dark Peak
Walking in Derbyshire
Walking in the Peak District
  — White Peak East
  — White Peak West

SOUTHERN ENGLAND
20 Classic Sportive Rides in South East England
20 Classic Sportive Rides in South West England
Bikepacking — South East Gravel
Cycling in the Cotswolds
Mountain Biking on the North Downs
South West Coast Path Map Booklet
  — Vol 1: Minehead to St Ives
  — Vol 2: St Ives to Plymouth
  — Vol 3: Plymouth to Poole
Suffolk Coast and Heath Walks
The Cotswold Way
The Cotswold Way Map Booklet
The Kennet and Avon Canal
The Lea Valley Walk
The Lea Valley Walk
The North Downs Way
North Downs Way Map Booklet
The Peddars Way and Norfolk Coast Path
The Pilgrims' Way
The Ridgeway National Trail
The Ridgeway Map Booklet
The South Downs Way
The South Downs Way Map Booklet
The Thames Path
The Thames Path Map Booklet
The Two Moors Way
Two Moors Way Map Booklet
Walking Hampshire's Test Way
Walking in Essex
Walking in Kent
Walking in London
Walking in Norfolk
Walking in the Chilterns
Walking in the Cotswolds
Walking in the Isles of Scilly
Walking in the New Forest
Walking in the North Wessachs Downs
Walking on Dartmoor
Walking on Guernsey
Walking on Jersey
Walking on the Isle of Wight
Walking the Dartmoor Way
Walking the Jurassic Coast
Walking the Sarsen Way
Walking the South West Coast Path
Walks in the South Downs National Park

WALES AND WELSH BORDERS
Cycle Touring in Wales
Cycling Lon Las Cymru
Great Mountain Days in Snowdonia
Hillwalking in Shropshire
Mountain Walking in Snowdonia
Offa's Dyke Path
Offa's Dyke Map Booklet
Scrambles in Snowdonia
Snowdonia: 30 Low-level and Easy Walks
  — North
  — South
The Cambrian Way
The Pembrokeshire Coast Path
Pembrokeshire Coast Path Map Booklet
The Snowdonia Way
The Wye Valley Walk
Walking Glyndwr's Way
Walking in Carmarthenshire
Walking in Gower
Walking in Pembrokeshire
Walking in the Brecon Beacons
Walking on Gower
Walking the Severn Way
Walking the Shropshire Way
Walking the Wales Coast Path

SHORT WALKS SERIES
15 Short Walks in Dumfries and Galloway
15 Short Walks in Perthshire North — Pitlochry, Aberfeldy and Dunkeld
15 Short Walks in the Scottish Borders
15 Short Walks in the Trossachs — Callander and Aberfoyle
15 Short Walks on the Isle of Mull
15 Short Walks on the Isle of Skye

- 15 Short Walks on the Orkney Islands
- 15 Short Walks on the Shetland Islands
- 15 Short Walks Hadrian's Wall
- 15 Short Walks in the Lake District
  — Keswick, Borrowdale and Buttermere
  — Windermere Ambleside and Grasmere
  — Coniston and Langdale
- 15 Short Walks in Arnside and Silverdale
- 15 Short Walks in the Ribble Valley
- 15 Short Walks in Nidderdale
- 15 Short Walks in Northumberland — Wooler, Rothbury, Alnwick and the coast
- 15 Short Walks in the Yorkshire Dales
  — Grassington, Skipton, Malham and Ilkley
  — Sedbergh, Kirkby Lonsdale and Ingleton
- 15 Short Walks in the Peak District — Bakewell and the White Peak
- 15 Short Walks in the Peak District — Edale and the Hope Valley
- 15 Short Walks on the Malvern Hills
- 15 Short Walks Cheddar and the Mendips
- 15 Short Walks in Cornwall
  — Newquay and the North Coast
  — Falmouth and the Lizard
  — Land's End and Penzance
- 15 Short Walks in Norfolk — Broads and Coast
- 15 Short Walks in South Devon — Salcombe, Brixham and the coast
- 15 Short Walks in the South Downs — Brighton, Eastbourne and Arundel
- 15 Short Walks in the Surrey Hills
- 15 Short Walks on Dartmoor North — Okehampton and Chagford
- 15 Short Walks on Dartmoor South — Ivybridge and Princetown
- 15 Short Walks on Exmoor
- 15 Short Walks on the Isle of Wight
- 15 Short Walks Winchester
- 15 Short Walks in Bannau Brycheiniog — Brecon Beacons
- 15 Short Walks in Pembrokeshire — Tenby and the south
- 15 Short Walks in the Forest of Dean

SCOTLAND

- Ben Nevis and Glen Coe
- Cycling in the Hebrides
- Cycling in the Hebrides
- Cycling the North Coast 500
- Great Mountain Days in Scotland
- Mountain Biking in Southern and Central Scotland
- Mountain Biking in West and North West Scotland
- Not the West Highland Way: A Mountain High Way
- Scotland
- Scotland's Best Small Mountains
- Scottish Wild Country Backpacking
- Skye Munros
- Skye's Cuillin Ridge Traverse
- The Borders Abbeys Way
- The Hebridean Way
- The Hebrides
- The Isle of Skye
- The Skye Trail
- The Southern Upland Way
- The West Highland Way
- West Highland Way Map Booklet
- Walking Ben Lawers, Rannoch and Atholl
- Walking in the Cairngorms
- Walking in the Pentland Hills
- Walking in the Scottish Borders
- Walking in the Southern Uplands
- Walking in Torridon, Fisherfield, Fannichs and An Teallach
- Walking Loch Lomond and the Trossachs
- Walking on Arran
- Walking on Harris and Lewis
- Walking on Jura, Islay and Colonsay
- Walking on Mull, Coll and Tiree
- Walking on Rum and the Small Isles
- Walking on the Orkney and Shetland Isles
- Walking on Uist and Barra
- Walking Rum and the Small Isles
- Walking the Cape Wrath Trail
- Walking the Corbetts
  Vol 1 — South of the Great Glen
  Vol 2 — North of the Great Glen
- Walking the Fife Pilgrim Way
- Walking the Galloway Hills
- Walking the Great Glen Way
- Walking the Great Glen Way Map Booklet
- Walking the John o' Groats Trail
- Walking the Munros
  Vol 1 — Southern, Central and Western Highlands
  Vol 2 — Northern Highlands and the Cairngorms
- Winter Climbs in the Cairngorms
- Winter Climbs: Ben Nevis and Glen Coe

ALPS CROSS-BORDER ROUTES

- 100 Hut Walks in the Alps
- Alpine Ski Mountaineering Vol 1 — Western Alps
- Hiking the Tour of Monte Rosa
- The Karnischer Höhenweg
- The Tour of the Bernina
- Trail Running — Chamonix and the Mont Blanc region
- Trekking Chamonix to Zermatt
- Trekking in the Alps
- Trekking in the Silvretta and Ratikon Alps
- Trekking Munich to Venice
- Trekking the Tour du Mont Blanc
- Tour du Mont Blanc Map Booklet
- Walking in the Alps

FRANCE, BELGIUM AND LUXEMBOURG

- Camino de Santiago — Via Podiensis
- Chamonix Mountain Adventures
- Cycling London to Paris
- Cycling the Canal de la Garonne
- Cycling the Canal du Midi
- Mont Blanc Walks
- Mountain Adventures in the Maurienne
- Short Treks on Corsica
- The GR5 Trail — Through the French Alps
- The GR5 Trail — Vosges and Jura
- The Moselle Cycle Route
- Trekking in the Vanoise
- Trekking the Cathar Way
- Trekking the GR10
- Trekking the GR20 Corsica
- Trekking the Robert Louis Stevenson Trail
- Via Ferratas of the French Alps
- Walking in Provence — East
- Walking in Provence — West
- Walking in the Auvergne
- Walking in the Briançonnais
- Walking in the Dordogne
- Walking in the Haute Savoie: North
- Walking in the Haute Savoie: South
- Walking on Corsica
- Walking the Brittany Coast Path
- The GR5 Trail — Benelux and Lorraine
- Walking in the Ardennes
- The River Loire Cycle Route
- The River Rhone Cycle Route
- Cycling the Route des Grandes Alpes

PYRENEES AND FRANCE/SPAIN CROSS-BORDER ROUTES

- Shorter Treks in the Pyrenees
- The Pyrenean Haute Route
- The Pyrenees
- Trekking the Cami dels Bons Homes
- Trekking the GR11 Trail
- Walks and Climbs in the Pyrenees

SPAIN AND PORTUGAL

- Camino de Santiago: Camino Frances
- Coastal Walks in Andalucia
- Costa Blanca Mountain Adventures
- Cycling the Camino de Santiago
- Mountain Walking in Mallorca
- Mountain Walking in Southern Catalunya
- Spain's Sendero Historico: The GR1
- The Andalucian Coast to Coast Walk
- The Camino del Norte and Camino Primitivo
- The Camino Ingles and Ruta do Mar
- The Mountains Around Nerja
- The Mountains of Ronda and Grazalema
- The Sierras of Extremadura
- Trekking in Mallorca
- Trekking in the Canary Islands
- Trekking the GR7 in Andalucia
- Walking and Trekking in the Sierra Nevada
- Walking in Andalucia
- Walking in Catalunya — Barcelona
- Walking in Catalunya — Girona Pyrenees
- Walking in the Picos de Europa
- Walking La Via de la Plata and Camino Sanabres
- Walking on Gran Canaria
- Walking on La Gomera and El Hierro
- Walking on La Palma
- Walking on Lanzarote and Fuerteventura

Walking on Tenerife
Walking on the Costa Blanca
Walking the Camino dos Faros
Portugal's Rota Vicentina
The Camino Portugues
Walking in Portugal
Walking in the Algarve
Walking in the Algarve
Walking on Madeira
Walking on the Azores
Cycling the Ruta Via de la Plata

SWITZERLAND

Switzerland's Jura Crest Trail
The Swiss Alps
Tour of the Jungfrau Region
Trekking the Swiss Via Alpina
Walking in Arolla and Zinal
Walking in the Bernese Oberland — Jungfrau region
Walking in the Engadine — Switzerland
Walking in Ticino
Walking in Zermatt and Saas-Fee

GERMANY

Hiking and Cycling in the Black Forest
The Danube Cycleway Vol 1
The Rhine Cycle Route
The Westweg
Walking in the Bavarian Alps
The Elbe Cycle Route

POLAND, SLOVAKIA, ROMANIA, HUNGARY AND BULGARIA

The Danube Cycleway Vol 2
The High Tatras
The Mountains of Romania

SCANDINAVIA, ICELAND AND GREENLAND

Hiking in Norway
— North
— South
Trekking the Kungsleden
Trekking in Greenland — The Arctic Circle Trail
Walking and Trekking in Iceland

SLOVENIA, CROATIA, SERBIA, MONTENEGRO AND ALBANIA

Hiking Slovenia's Juliana Trail
Mountain Biking in Slovenia
The Islands of Croatia
The Julian Alps of Slovenia
The Mountains of Montenegro
The Peaks of the Balkans Trail
The Slovene Mountain Trail
Walking in Slovenia: The Karavanke
Walking the Julian Alps of Slovenia
Walks and Treks in Croatia

ITALY

Alta Via 1 — Trekking in the Dolomites
Alta Via 2 — Trekking in the Dolomites
Day Walks in the Dolomites
Italy's Grande Traversata delle Alpi
Ski Touring and Snowshoeing in the Dolomites
The Way of St Francis: Via di Francesco
Trekking Gran Paradiso: Alta Via 2
Trekking in the Apennines
Trekking the Giants' Trail: Alta Via 1 through the Italian Pennine Alps
Via Ferratas of the Italian Dolomites
— Vol 1
— Vol 2
Walking Gran Paradiso National Park
Walking in Abruzzo
Walking in Italy's Cinque Terre
Walking in Italy's Stelvio National Park
Walking in Sicily
Walking in the Aosta Valley
Walking in the Dolomites
Walking in Tuscany
Walking in Umbria
Walking Lake Como and Maggiore
Walking Lake Garda and Iseo
Walking on the Amalfi Coast
Walking the Cammino Materano
Walking the Via Francigena Pilgrim Route
— Part 1
— Part 2
— Part 3
— Part 4
Walks and Treks in the Maritime Alps

IRELAND

The Wild Atlantic Way and Western Ireland
Walking the Kerry Way
Walking the Wicklow Way

INTERNATIONAL CHALLENGES, COLLECTIONS AND ACTIVITIES

Europe's High Points
Pocket First Aid and Wilderness Medicine

AUSTRIA

Innsbruck Mountain Adventures
Trekking Austria's Adlerweg
Trekking in Austria's Hohe Tauern
Trekking in Austria's Stubai Alps
Trekking in Austria's Zillertal Alps
Walking in Austria
Walking in the Salzkammergut: the Austrian Lake District

MEDITERRANEAN

Trekking in Greece
Walking and Trekking in Zagori
Walking and Trekking on Corfu
Walking on the Greek Islands — the Cyclades
Walking in Cyprus
Walking on Malta

HIMALAYA

8000 metres
Annapurna
Everest: A Trekker's Guide
Trekking in the Indian Himalayas
Trekking in the Karakoram

NORTH AMERICA

Hiking and Cycling the California Missions Trail
Hiking the Pacific Crest Trail
The John Muir Trail

SOUTH AMERICA

Aconcagua and the Southern Andes
Hiking and Biking Peru's Inca Trails
Trekking in Torres del Paine

AFRICA

Climbing Toubkal
Kilimanjaro
Walking in the Drakensberg
Walks and Scrambles in the Moroccan Anti-Atlas

NEW ZEALAND AND AUSTRALIA

Hiking the Overland Track

CHINA, JAPAN AND ASIA

Hiking and Trekking in the Japan Alps and Mount Fuji
Hiking in Hong Kong
Japan's Kumano Kodo Pilgrimage
Trekking in Bhutan
Trekking in Ladakh
Trekking in Tajikistan
Trekking in the Himalaya

TECHNIQUES

Fastpacking
The Mountain Hut Book

MINI GUIDES

Alpine Flowers
Navigation

MOUNTAIN LITERATURE

A Walk in the Clouds
Abode of the Gods
Fifty Years of Adventure
The Pennine Way — the Path, the People, the Journey
Unjustifiable Risk?

For full information on all our guides, books and eBooks,
visit our website:
www.cicerone.co.uk

CICERONE

Trust Cicerone to guide your next adventure, wherever it may be around the world...

Discover guides for hiking, mountain walking, backpacking, trekking, trail running, cycling and mountain biking, ski touring, climbing and scrambling in Britain, Europe and worldwide.

Connect with Cicerone online and find inspiration.

- buy books and ebooks
- articles, advice and trip reports
- GPX files and updates
- regular newsletter

cicerone.co.uk